ONLINE INFLUENCE

ONLINE INFLUENCE

Boost your results with proven behavioral science

Bas Wouters and Joris Groen

With the assistance of
Jaap Janssen Steenberg and Stijn Kling

© 2020 Joris Groen and Bas Wouters

Cover design: Studio Johan Nijhoff, Amsterdam
Interior layout: Holland Graphics, Amsterdam
Translation: Natalie Bowler-Geerinck, Rode, Verenigd Koninkrijk
Illustrations: Geertjan Tromp and Florence Hoogveld

ISBN 9798697006924
NUR 801/802

Subject to the exceptions laid down in or pursuant to the Dutch Copyright Act (Auteurswet), it is prohibited for anything in this publication to be copied, stored in a data file or made public, in any way or form, be it electronic, mechanical, by means of photocopies, recording or any other method without prior written permission from the authors.

No part of this book may be reproduced in any form, by print, photo print, microfilm or any means other without written permission from the authors.

"With their new book, Bas Wouters and Joris Groen have given a true gift to those of us who want to become more influential online. In one place, they have provided current, scientifically-based information on the most successful forms of behavior design, persuasive prompts, psychological motivators, practical applications, and more. I was particularly impressed with the book's advice on simple strategies for making online messaging more effective. For anyone working in online commerce, this book should not be missed."

Robert Cialdini
New York Times best selling author of Influence and Pre-Suasion

Content

INTRODUCTION	11
Online influence	13
PART 1 HOW TO DESIGN BEHAVIOR	17
What is behavior design?	19
The Fogg Behavior Model	27
Daniel Kahneman's two systems	33
Robert Cialdini's principles of persuasion	39
The ethical side	43
PART 2 HOW TO DESIGN A WINNING PROMPT	47
What is a prompt?	49
Attention	55
Competing prompts	63
Affordance	69
Name the desired behavior, literally	77
Curiosity	81
Exceptional benefit	87
Simple question	91
Unfinished journey	97
PART 3 HOW TO BOOST MOTIVATION	101
What is motivation?	103
Anticipatory enthusiasm	111

Appealing to basic needs	119
Social proof	123
Authority	131
Baby steps	137
Scarcity	145
Positive feedback	151
Loss aversion	155
Perceived value	161
Reasons why	165

PART 4 HOW TO INCREASE ABILITY — 169

What is ability?	171
Reduce options	177
Offer decision aid	183
Default, prefill and autocomplete	189
The Jenga technique	195
Remove distractions	201
Provide feedback	205
Offer reversibility	211
Page structure	215
Don't make me think	223
Familiarity	229
Expected effort	233
Making undesirable behavior more difficult	237

PART 5 HOW TO DESIGN CHOICES — 241

What is choice architecture?	243
Hobson + 1	247
Anchoring	253
Extreme aversion	257
Decoy	261
Nudging	267

PART 6 HOW TO APPLY BEHAVIORAL PSYCHOLOGY — 271

And now: how to put it all into practice	273
Online advertising	275
Display ads	279

Social media ads	289
Email ads	297
Search engine ads	313
Landing pages	317
Product detail pages	339
The checkout	353
Conversion research	375
Web analysis	381
Optimizing by experimenting	383
Behavior Design Roadmap	389
Checklists for the different applications	395
Acknowledgements	405
Reading suggestions	407
About the authors	409
Bibliography	411

Introduction

Most online visitors don't do what you want them to do

INTRODUCTION

Online influence

If you believe certain media, we are all a willing prey for online persuasion tricks. We are manipulated en masse, so the story goes, to click on banners, make commitments and order products that we don't really need. But the numbers paint a different picture: most website visitors, downloaders of apps and email recipients do not do what the makers want at all.

For example, extremely successful web shops make a sale to 'only' one in ten people visiting their website. And as an online advertiser you are already doing pretty well if one in a thousand people clicks on your banner. If this were the performance of a face-to-face sales person, their employers would probably not be too happy.

In other words, in the online world the dropouts outnumber the buyers. It's hardly surprising, when you think about it: after all, it is pretty incredible how we allow images, texts and buttons to persuade us to share our personal data, fill in our credit card number and make long-term commitments. All this, without any intervention from 'real' people we know or trust personally.

A world of difference
How you design your online environment can make a world of difference, as evidenced by the many successful experiments that we, and many others, have conducted. In this book, we want to share the knowledge we have gained with you. We will teach you how to use the science of behavior change or influencing to persuade many people online to do the behavior you want. This is what will happen:

- Ignoring becomes **responding**.
- Browsing becomes **buying**.
- Unsubscribing becomes **continued membership**.
- Dropping out becomes **keep going**.
- And "hmm" becomes **"yes"**.

Which will lead to:

- more online revenue;
- lower advertising costs;
- a higher conversion rate;
- more **satisfied customers**.

Satisfied customers

In our opinion, the latter (satisfied customers) equals 'sustainable' online persuasion. This is an important point, because online influence is unfortunately still associated with deception sometimes. We call this 'dark patterns': misleading design patterns that lead us to buy travel insurance when we don't want it, for example.

So that's not what we're going to do.

Not only for ethical reasons, but also because it is simply not how you achieve success in the long term.

As you will notice, online persuasion is mainly about making people even more enthusiastic than they already were. But definitely also about:

- helping them to make difficult choices;
- guiding them optimally in their decision whether or not to do business with you;
- simplifying the route to the goal.

This leads to more results and a higher appreciation of your online channel.

Science and practice

A lot of books and especially blogs have been written about online influencing. But in our opinion, they are still not practical and complete enough. They often assume a rather randomly chosen psychological theory or a common cognitive bias (irrational thinking pattern). This is often followed by well-meaning advice about what we could do to persuade people online.

It's a little bit like an architect picking a random law of physics and wondering how he might use it to design a complicated roof construction. This may not be the most efficient way.

> *"A designer who doesn't understand human psychologies is going to be no more successful than an architect who doesn't understand physics."*
>
> — JOE LEECH[1]

In this book, we are going to handle things differently. The online customer journey will serve as our starting point, and we will be with you every step of the way to tell you what psychological knowledge you need to get the most out of it. You will learn how to cleverly and tactically design your ads, landing pages, forms, checkouts and even thank-you pages using design principles, and *which* principle you should use *where* and *when*.

We will give you an approach that is based on science and has been tested in practice. We have achieved excellent results for many companies with this approach. Prior to that, we also failed spectacularly by applying the wrong methods. This is good news for you, because you won't have to make the same mistakes. You can start immediately with the insights from our forty years of combined experience in online influence: scientifically founded, proven in practice.

Fogg, Cialdini and Kahneman
The behavioral model of BJ Fogg, the founder of 'behavior design', plays a starring role. Although there are many models that *explain* behavior, this model actually helps you to *design* behavior. In addition, we gratefully draw on the work of persuasion psychologist Robert Cialdini, who has bundled years of research on persuasion mechanisms into seven powerful principles of persuasion. Another essential branch of psychology for online influencers is that of our unconscious, automatic brain, as described by psychologist, economist and Nobel laureate Daniel Kahneman. In this book, we explain his theory and teach you how to apply it in practice.

To complete the model, we have added many insights from our own online marketing practice, gained from many local and international clients, such as Mercedes-Benz, KLM, bol.com (the largest Dutch online retailer, comparable to Amazon).

Equipped with all these insights, you will be able to greatly increase your online influence and give your business a big boost.

Bas Wouters
Joris Groen

WHO IS THIS BOOK FOR?
We have written this book for all professionals who want to influence their (potential) customers' online behavior. So whether you are a web builder or UX designer, copywriter or graphic designer, entrepreneur, marketer or product manager: if you want to increase your online influence, you have come to the right place. From now on we will refer to you as a 'behavior designer'.

Part 1
How to design behavior

As of today you will design nothing but behavior

HOW TO DESIGN BEHAVIOR

What is behavior design?

Imagine that as the authors of this book, we get to choose a single rule for you to remember for the rest of your career. We wouldn't hesitate even for a second. We would pick the rule on the previous page.

'Designing behavior': it took us some time to get used to this word combination as well. You would typically design an advert, a website, a product. But 'designing behavior' sounds almost as if you can make people do anything you want. The founder of behavior design, BJ Fogg, has a much better definition, however. To him, behavior design means: getting people to do something they already want to do.

Hold on, you may be wondering, if people already want to do something, why would you need to persuade them? That is precisely where the problem lies. The fact that we *want* something does not automatically mean that we actually *do* it.

Behavior designers base their work on the following two important psychological truths:

- We don't often do things without being asked.
- If something becomes too hard, we give up quickly.

You may recognize this in yourself. Or you may prefer not to... After all, these are qualities we're not exactly proud of: being passive and not persevering.

Behavior designers don't judge this. They set up the (online) environment in such a way they break through the inactivity. They do this first of all with 'prompts' that alert their target group to the desired behavior. Second, they make behavior as easy as possible. They achieve this by removing barriers, like overly complicated click paths or unnecessary fields in a contact form. And thirdly, they try to give the motivation a temporary boost so that the target group is willing to overcome the barriers. After all, some behavior will always remain hard to do.

From web design to behavior design

When designing a new website, an online campaign or a landing page, newbie designers like to search for successful examples by others. These best practices form the basis for their design. The more experienced designers usually start by mapping out the user profile in detail and analyzing the 'tasks' they have to perform. Next, they design a website that facilitates user tasks. The positive user experience they are aiming for is the core of the user experience design field, usually abbreviated as 'UX design'.

If you want optimal online results, however, you need more than just user-friendliness to persuade people. The term 'user' is actually an unfortunate choice. This term suggests that there is a motivated person on the other side of the screen who has actually already decided to do business with you and use your website. Also take a critical look at the term 'customer journey': what do you mean: customer? That remains to be seen.

Whether your visitors eventually become customers depends very much on the context they are in. Often, they are not sure if they want to order, or to order from you and not your competitor. And who knows, they might drop out because they have doubts after all. Or get distracted. Or think the order process is too complicated. This means we should not only facilitate our potential customers, but also persuade them step by step – behavior after behavior – towards conversion.

This is why behavior designers prefer the terms 'visitors' or 'potential customers' to 'users'. This means a change in perspective. As a behavior designer, you start from the behavior you want to see and create a route full of persuasion tactics to achieve this behavior. You also understand that you are battling with competing temptations that, just like you, are fighting for your visitors' time and attention.

This is why behavior design is so much more than a simple 'sauce' of persuasion on an existing website. It is a fundamentally different view of online design. It is a view that leads to different solutions than simply copying best practices or relying exclusively on user-friendliness.

An example

Let's take a practical example. See the mailing Joris and his team at Buyerminds designed for KLM. It's the email people receive two weeks before departure.

The desired behavior – or rather, the collection of 'micro-behaviors' – is that recipients open the email, read the intro, go through the checklist and click on a component that is relevant to them, like ordering additional luggage.

As you can read in the captions, we have used scientific insight in eight places to influence these behaviors. And successfully so: emails based on this design were opened more often and generated more clicks to the website.

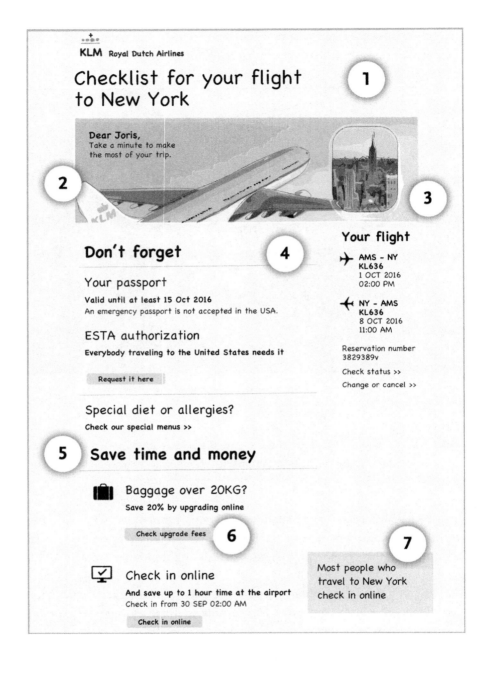

1 Arouse curiosity
Checklist is a word that makes people curious. The original email said, "Prepare for your trip." That's less of an incentive to read.

2 Reduce the expected effort
The effort that we expect to have to put in partly determines whether we want to start doing something. By indicating that the checklist only takes a minute to complete, we encourage more people to read.

3 Create anticipatory enthusiasm
By visualizing the view of the New York skyline from the plane, we allow the readers to (almost literally) look forward to the trip they had just booked. Anticipating the future reward helps to get people into active mode.

4 Reduce mental effort
Facilitating behavior increases the chance that we will actually perform it. The layout of the mail minimizes the mental effort. For example, we keep important information, such as the flight number and departure time, separate from the checklist. This helps readers to easily find this information (or easily ignore it). This clear visual hierarchy allows us to communicate the structure of the checklist at a glance.

5 Give reasons why
When you explicitly provide a reason for a certain behavior, chances of that behavior happening increase. In this case, saving time and money is obviously a good reason to upgrade your luggage and check in online.

6 Ask for minor commitments
It's easier to take small steps than big ones. To interest readers in an upsell or upgrade, we propose only a small commitment ('Check upgrade fees') instead of a big one ('Buy now!').

7 Provide social proof
If someone asks us to do certain behaviors, we subconsciously check whether other people are doing those behaviors as well. When we see this, we call it 'social proof'. That is why we show people that it is perfectly normal behavior to check in online.

The best profession

The power of behavior design is that you leave nothing to chance. The desired behavior is central to everything. If you don't do this, your design is likely to be counterproductive because it makes things more difficult. But if you start working from this perspective as of today, you will be extremely valuable as a web builder or UX designer, as a copywriter or graphic designer, as an entrepreneur, marketer, product manager or whatever role you may play in convincing your target group online. It's the best job ever, in our view.

CONVERSION

In this book, we often use the word 'conversion'. As an online professional, you undoubtedly know what that term means, but for the newbies in this field, we would like to say a few words about it. The conversion ratio is the measure of persuasiveness in the online world: the number of visitors who do the desired behavior, divided by the total number of visitors, expressed as a percentage:

$$\text{Conversion ratio (\%)} = \frac{\text{Number of visitors doing the desired behavior}}{\text{Total number of visitors}} \times 100$$

Suppose: in a web shop, 5 out of 100 visitors leave a review. The conversion ratio is 5 percent. If, after your redesign, 10 out of 100 visitors leave a review, your conversion rate is 10 percent. In other words: your conversion has doubled. On the surface, it seems as if you have 'only' (for example) adjusted the header, the image and the call-to-action button, but by doing so you have first and foremost changed the behavior of your visitors: a boost for your online business!

B = MAP

HOW TO DESIGN BEHAVIOR

The Fogg Behavior Model

Right, so we are going to *design* behavior. To do so, we turn to BJ Fogg. In 2009, this American behavioral scientist came up with a model that allows us to examine behavior and behavioral change in a structured way. Unparalleled in its applicability, it is worth its weight in gold for you as a behavior designer.

BJ Fogg is a professor at Stanford University, one of the most prestigious universities in the United States. He researches human behavior and what exactly it takes to change it. There were some big names among his students. How about Mike Krieger, a co-founder of Instagram? Or Tristan Harris, the founder of the Center of Human Technology (CHT), the movement that fights, among other things, addiction to social media? In addition to teaching, Fogg advises the business community about applying behavioral psychology.

But what matters here is that he has developed the model that now bears his name: the Fogg Behavior Model.[2] This makes him the inventor of the discipline we now call 'behavior design'. The starting point of his model is that people do not just start exhibiting certain behaviors of their own accord. According to Fogg, three conditions must be met:

- There has to be a prompt to start the behavior.
- At the time of the prompt, the motivation must be high enough.
- At the time of the prompt, the behavior we ask for must be simple enough.

Trinity
Let's start by zooming in on the prompt. What exactly is a prompt? A prompt is something that asks or reminds us to do certain behavior. Think, for example,

of the sound of your alarm clock: this is your call to wake up in the morning. Or take the push notification on the screen of your smartphone: it invites you to open an app. According to Fogg, there are not many behaviors that are not triggered by an external request.

If you are already familiar with the Fogg Behavior Model, you will know that Fogg initially used the term 'trigger'. That term proved to be open to too many interpretations. That is why he now calls it a 'prompt', and so do we. In the *Prompts* section, we will elaborate on this, but for now it is enough to remember that almost every behavior starts with a prompt.

The Fogg Behavior Model says that a prompt will only lead to actual behavior if the motivation and ability to do that behavior are sufficient. We will also deal with these concepts in detail in the *Motivation* and *Ability* sections. For now, it's enough to know that motivation is about how *much* a person wants something, and ability about how *easy* it is to do behavior.

Without sufficient motivation and ability plus a prompt, no behavior will occur, Fogg teaches us. If we look at these three factors systematically, we will make much more progress with our online design than if we look for a 'nice template for a landing page' or the 'top 10 best-scoring advertisements'.

Take a look at the graph. Motivation, ability and the prompt are a crucial trinity. The vertical axis indicates motivation, the horizontal axis the ability. If both are high enough and above the action line, behavior will occur the moment we observe the prompt. If the motivation and ability are not high enough, and thus remain below the action line, a prompt will not lead to the desired behavior.

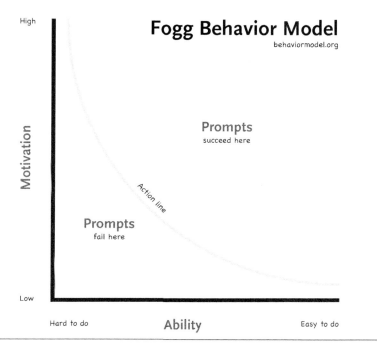

B = MAP
To initiate behavior a person must be sufficiently motivated (motivation) and the behavior must be easy enough (ability). That's the moment to introduce your prompt.

Interaction

This does not mean that both the motivation and the ability have to be very high at the time of the prompt. There is an interaction. For example, look at the top left corner of the graph. If you are extremely motivated, it does not matter much how difficult the behavior is. After all, you are prepared to overcome 'all' obstacles, no matter how complicated, expensive or difficult the behavior is. For example, if you want to buy tickets to a concert by your favorite artist, which usually sells out in no time, you will happily sit with your laptop for an hour and keep updating your browser for a chance to get those tickets. In that case, your high motivation compensates for the limited ability.

The reverse is also true, of course: if your motivation is very low, you can still be persuaded to do something by greatly increasing the ability. See the lower right corner of the graph. For example, if you're walking in a shopping area, there's always one of those friendly students around who wants to give you a free newspaper. Even if you have a newspaper at home and you don't like the one on offer, you will still accept it sometimes. Why? The ability is enormous: it is almost easier to accept the newspaper than to refuse.

If one factor is extra strong, it may be sufficient to compensate for the other factor if it is less strong. Behavior design is all about that interplay.

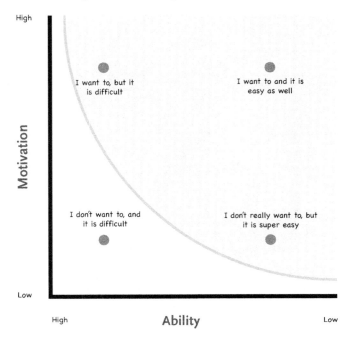

Good to know: of the three factors of the Fogg Behavior Model, motivation is the most difficult to influence. In other words, it is best to try to change behavior in situations where there is already some motivation. In our section on motivation, we therefore mainly assume *motivation-enhancing* influence, and not influencing unwilling people. As a behavior designer, you can design prompts and make behavior easy.

Model as the basis of this book

The Fogg Behavior Model is your ideal guide to behavior design. That's why we used it for the layout of this book. We cover all 37 design principles in the light of the three factors of the model:

- principles that make prompts more effective;
- principles that increase motivation;
- principles that increase ability.

When you wonder how you can stimulate a certain behavior – and thus achieve more conversion – as a behavior designer you systematically work your way through these three factors. The same applies to the thought experiment with WhatsApp (see the experiment below). By doing research or thinking logically, you can pretty much estimate what is wrong with it: motivation, ability or a clear prompt. Or maybe two or even three factors. You examine which factor you can improve the fastest and easiest. Tip: this is usually the prompt, followed by ability. And as we've mentioned: motivation is the most difficult.

THOUGHT EXPERIMENT: WHATSAPPING WITH YOUR PARTNER
Why not try this thought experiment to better understand the Fogg Behavior Model.

Imagine that you have asked your partner to go out for dinner via WhatsApp. You can see the familiar blue check marks appear, so your message has been read. But after half an hour you still have no response. While the behavior you want is: answering your message.

Ask yourself what might be going on: not by speculating wildly, but by applying the Fogg Behavior Model. Where are you going wrong?

- *Is the prompt missing?*
- *Is it lack of ability (too difficult)?*
- *Or is it lack of motivation?*

When, during our workshops and lectures, we ask who thinks it's because of motivation, hands invariably go up en masse. Apparently, people are inclined to doubt people's motivation when the desired behavior does not occur. However, as a behavior designer, you have to let go of this assumption. Who knows, it might have been difficult to answer at the time. Or maybe your partner didn't even read the message. After all, the check marks also turn blue if the screen is opened briefly while you are doing something else.

In short: there are three possibilities why the desired behavior, answering a message, does not occur: lack of a prompt, lack of ability and/or lack of motivation. If you do this with your website, online campaign or banner, for example, you are already taking a huge step towards successful behavior design.

95 percent of our choices
is influenced by our
unconscious brain

HOW TO DESIGN BEHAVIOR

Daniel Kahneman's two systems

In 2002, behavioral psychologist Daniel Kahneman was awarded the Nobel Prize in Economics. It was hardly surprising, because with his research at the interface of psychology and economics, he has made us see behavior in a new way. He did this mainly by showing that we act much less rationally than we always thought, and often still think.

It has long been known that we have two ways of thinking: a fast way and a slow way. Psychology sometimes refers to them as 'System 1' and 'System 2':

- System 1: our unconscious thinking brain
  This is a fast, automatic and intuitive way of thinking that requires hardly any effort.

- System 2: our conscious thinking brain
  This is a slow, well-considered and rational way of thinking that requires a lot of effort.

Various studies have shown that a whopping 95 percent of our actions, judgments and choices are unconsciously handled by System 1.[3] And that's a good thing. Take a look at the list below from Kahneman's work.[4]

Typical System 1-actions, in order of complexity:

- showing aversion to a frightening image;
- solving the sum 2 + 2 = ?;
- reading the text on a billboard;
- driving a car on an empty road;
- understanding simple sentences.

These are all simple actions that we simply have to perform on autopilot. Every day, we make hundreds or sometimes thousands of decisions, depending on exactly what we mean by a decision (psychologists haven't managed to agree on this yet). What we do know for sure is that there are too many choices to consciously make with our slow System 2. We would go mad in no time. In fact, we wouldn't be able to cope at all. We simply don't have enough time and energy.

But luckily we also have System 1, which handles 95 percent of all these decisions for us. As a result, System 2 has enough time and energy for the things that really need our attention.

Typical System 2 actions, in order of complexity:

- bracing yourself for the start of a race;
- being on the lookout for a woman with gray hair;
- assessing the appropriateness of your behavior in a certain social setting;
- parking in a tight parking space;
- judging the accuracy of a complex reasoning.

As you can see, these are all actions that we can only perform consciously.

As a behavior designer, you have to understand the interaction between the two systems. System 1 determines whether a prompt is important enough to respond to it. Moreover, as Kahneman discovered, System 1 often uses shortcuts or cognitive biases: lightning-fast assumptions based on which it makes decisions. A few examples:

- If something is expensive, it is better than something that is cheap.
- If something is popular, it's better than something that is unpopular.
- If the option in the middle is better than those at the extreme ends of the spectrum, it is safer than the other choices.
- When something is nearly finished, it is valuable and you need to act quickly.
- If you get a quick reward for something, it is fun.

That is, of course, not always true, but often it is. That's why System 1 bases its choices on such shortcuts.

First System 1, then System 2

Kahneman emphasizes that System 1 and 2 are both always active, except when we are asleep. System 1 runs automatically, while System 2 is in a sort of sleep mode. System 1 generates impressions, ideas, intentions and feelings, of which only the most striking are transferred to System 2 for further inspection. And that's where the shortcuts come in: when assessing your online environment, it is the shortcuts of System 1 that influence the feelings and opinions of your visitor in no time.

If you are a behavior designer and use the Fogg Behavior Model, it is crucial that you take this into account. We'll take you through the three factors one by one.

System 1 and prompts
System 1 processes an incredible amount of information. That is why it is best to address this system with a prompt at its own level: similar to that of a 7-year-old child (see the box). If your prompt is good, you create enough stopping power and the information can be transferred to System 2.

System 1 and motivation
As Kahneman wrote: "System 1 runs the show, that's the one you want to move." So if you understand which shortcuts put System 1 in motion, you can increase the motivation of your potential customer's motivation.

System 1 and ability
Making behavior easier is done by having micro decisions and actions carried out by System 1: if we let our automatic and unconscious brain do the work, it doesn't feel like mental effort.

A REPTILE OR A 7-YEAR-OLD CHILD?

If you have studied this field before, you may have read that System 1 is also called the 'reptilian brain'. But, as you've just read in the list, counting and reading also fall under System 1 operations. That's why we think the term 'reptilian brain' is kind of inadequate. It is better to think of a 7-year-old child when designing for System 1. It can solve basic math problems and read simple sentences, but is not yet able to reason logically.

Reciprocity
Commitment & consistency
Social proof
Liking
Authority
Scarcity
Unity

HOW TO DESIGN BEHAVIOR

Robert Cialdini's principles of persuasion

BJ Fogg has given us a model with which we can tackle behavioral influencing in a structured manner. But what about Cialdini's principles of persuasion? Aren't they the basis of persuasion? People often ask us this question. We have given the Cialdini principles a place within the Fogg Behavior Model.

The American professor of psychology and marketing Robert Cialdini is a heavyweight in his field. He is the most quoted scientist in the field of persuasion. It's hardly surprising: he researched persuasion principles for years and made them transparent. And also, successfully applicable.

He did this through literature and clinical research, and by going undercover with car dealers, door-to-door salesmen and advertisers, among others. Based on all this research, he concluded that there are seven principles of persuasion we can use to influence others. He describes six of them in his book *Influence – The psychology of persuasion*, which has sold more than four million copies worldwide.[5] He later added a seventh principle (see box).

Cialdini and Fogg
We cover the most practically applicable principles to use 'online' in the *Motivation* section. After all, this is the part of the Fogg Behavior Model that shows the Cialdini principles to their best advantage.

In case you have never heard of Cialdini, or missed his book, we've included a list of his principles (see box).

THE SEVEN PRINCIPLES OF CIALDINI

Reciprocity
We feel obliged to give back what we received earlier. That is why it is smart to give your visitors something before you invite them to the desired behavior.[6]

Commitment and consistency
We like to act consistently with our previous actions and positions. That is why it is smart to use small steps to entice your visitors towards the desired behavior. (See chapter *Baby-steps*.)

Social proof
In case of doubt and choice overload, we allow ourselves to be guided by the people around us. That is why it is smart to show that others also do the desired behavior. (See chapter *Social Proof*)

Liking
We're more likely to say yes to people we like. That is why it is smart to give your visitors a reason to like you, for example by giving compliments and emphasizing similarities.[7]

Authority
We trust people who have more knowledge and expertise than we do. That is why it is smart to demonstrate that you have knowledge and skills on which your visitors can build. (See chapter *Authority*.)

Scarcity
We attach more value to things when they are limited or only available temporarily. That is why it is smart to make something extra attractive by emphasizing its limited availability, in terms of quantity or time. (See chapter *Scarcity*.)

Unity
We are more likely to trust people who are part of the same group as ourselves. That is why it is smart to create a sense of togetherness, or to use the unity that we feel with others.[8]

Persuading is not the same as misleading

HOW TO DESIGN BEHAVIOR
The ethical side

And now for the elephant in the room. Here's a question that everyone sometimes asks or should ask themselves: is applying behavior design ethical? You may have heard examples of websites that manipulate or downright mislead their visitors. When do you cross the line?

The line between persuading and misleading does not always appear easy to determine. What some find misleading, such as raising prices one week before Black Friday, is healthy commercial behavior to others. And then there are also standards, values and laws to consider that vary per country or culture.

Content ...
Nevertheless, there is a generally accepted test that can confirm that you are being ethical. Cialdini lists three criteria that you must meet to act ethically: truth, sincerity and wisdom. To this end, he formulated the following practical questions:

- *Am I telling the truth?*
  Am I giving my customer the correct information? Would I also give this information to my mother or my best friend? If I say that there are only three seats available, is that really true?

- *Am I presenting my request sincerely?*
  Am I not selling nonsense like that famous supermarket in the United States? It offered water, with the word "SALE' in large print on a board. The offer was: from $~~0.69~~ for $0.69. Sales increased until the customers realized that they were being fooled structurally.

- *Is it wise to make this request?*
  If a customer says yes to my request now, will they want to do business with me in the future?

If you can answer all three questions positively, you are taking your first step towards a win-win situation.

... and form

Ethical aspects are not only related to the content of your message. The same applies to the form of your message. Here too, you can ask yourself a few questions:

- *Am I not using a shape or pattern in a different way than is actually intended?*
  A play button starts a video, it should not send you to another website. A badge app symbol indicates that there is a new message, and is not intended to simply attract attention.

- *Am I not deliberately creating confusion?*
  Placing a check mark means you're choosing something. Not that you are making a choice against something.

👎 **Don't**

- *Am I not hiding something important?*
  You shouldn't make impactful information so small that no one is able to find it or read it.

  👎 **Don't**

If you can also answer these questions with 'yes', you are using your design in the right way and you will not lose the trust of your customer.

Part 2

How to design a winning prompt

HOW TO DESIGN A WINNING PROMPT

What is a prompt?

Almost every behavior starts with a prompt. This includes online behavior. In this chapter, we discuss in detail what a prompt is and how to design effective prompts as a behavior designer.

The previous chapter already contained a short definition of a prompt:

A prompt is something that asks us to do certain behavior or reminds us to do so.

Examples include the sound of your alarm clock and push notifications on the screen of your smartphone. Both are invitations to behavior: waking up and opening an app.

For online design, you can think of the following examples:

- the push notification that asks you to open a news article;
- the badge app symbol that asks you to open an app;
- the header above a text that encourages you to read the article;
- the 'Add to shopping basket' button that asks you to put the product of your choice in your shopping basket;
- the blinking cursor in the first field of the registration form that asks you to start filling the form.

If you look at your online environment from this perspective, you'll see that all online behavior also starts with a prompt. Prompt-reinforcing principles lead to more visitors doing what you want, which will increase your conversion rate.

A chain of prompts

Prompts often do not stand alone. The behavior that we ultimately want to achieve consists mostly of a series of micro behaviors. And every micro behavior is triggered by its own prompt. In the following example, we have broken down 'sign up' behavior into micro behaviors:

Micro behavior	The prompt that calls for this behavior
Visiting the landing page	The advertisement on a website with the text 'Sign up now' and the 'Click here' button
Reading the text	The header above the text
Scrolling down	The fact that the text is not yet finished and continues outside of your field of vision
Starting registration	The 'Register' button on the landing page
Entering your email address	The instruction 'Enter your email address' and the empty field below with a blinking cursor
Sending the registration form	The 'Send' button at the bottom of the form

Armed with the principles in this chapter, you can design an effective prompt for each micro behavior to increase your chances of success step by step.

Prompt Strategies

It is important to understand that the first prompt is often the hardest. After all, this is the prompt that should lure people away from what they are doing at that moment. To achieve this, you are going to need more than just a dry call to action. Further in this section, we describe four prompt strategies that are suitable for this purpose:

- Curiosity – making people extra curious;
- Exceptional benefit – making people extra greedy;
- Simple question – starting a nice conversation;
- Unfinished journey – building on the task that people are already performing.

Together with the prompt, these strategies provide a considerable motivation boost. Incidentally, we consciously refer to four 'strategies', because you really have to choose which strategy you are going to use for your prompt.

Prompt versus message

Still, there's more to our explanation of the prompt. In practice, we have noticed that the difference between a prompt and a persuasive message for marketing or advertising purposes is not always clear, for example. This is hardly surprising because often they both contain text. However, the purpose of a prompt is different from that of a message:

- A prompt aims to *immediately prompt behavior*.
- A message aims to get *a certain idea into people's minds*.

A few differences between a prompt and a persuasive message are:

Persuasive message	Prompt
Intended to change your attitude. In other words: how and what you think about something.	Intended to immediately trigger behavior.
Intended to think about it often and for a long time: • double meaning • play on words • attention span • originality • humor	Intended to be understood quickly: • few words • simple words • unequivocal • recognizability
Intended to be remembered: • rhyme • alliteration • repetition	Intended to lure you away from what you are doing: • curiosity • exceptional benefit • simple question • unfinished journey

A message does not necessarily require immediate behavior (see left column). After all, the purpose of a message is to make people think about it for a long time, so that they actually remember the message. Take billboards and commercial breaks on TV, for example: they are purely intended to 'upload' a company name, a brand, or a product into our brain. By delivering the message in an original way, for example, with a double entendre or a play on words, the recipients will continue to think about it a little longer. And if you use rhyme or repetition, you increase the chances of people remembering your message.

This is not the case for prompts (see right column). It should simply trigger behavior. That is why a prompt must be understood immediately. Recognizability contributes to this, but beware: originality can be counterproductive, especially when the text is not easy to understand. Recipients don't have to remember a prompt either.

For the remainder of this book, we will not be talking about persuasive messages that you want to get into your target group's head through mass media. After all, that's a different area of expertise.

Other things you will learn

In the rest of this chapter, we will get down to business. We start with how to draw attention and eliminate competing prompts. Then we'll show you how to improve affordance. In other words: how to make it clear to your visitors what they should do when they see a prompt. Next, we will discuss the notion that you can expect more results if you use verbs to literally tell your visitors what they should do. And finally, we will teach you how to use the four prompt strategies so that your visitors stop what they are doing.

Attention
Attract attention with something that moves, something that stands out, a person, an animal or an emotion.

Competing prompts
Limit the number of prompts, preferably to one, or make the most important prompt stand out the most.

Affordance
Make it clear in a millisecond that your prompt is clickable (or scrollable or swipeable).

Name the desired behavior, literally
Literally name the desired behavior, using the imperative form.

Curiosity
Persuade your visitors to click by making them very curious.

Exceptional benefit
Persuade your visitors with an offer that seems too good to be true.

Simple question
Ask your visitors a question that is easy to understand and easy to answer.

Unfinished journey
Frame the desired behavior as a logical next step.

If your prompt is not seen, it's 'game over' straight away

HOW TO DESIGN A WINNING PROMPT

Attention

A prompt is only a prompt if recipients actually see it. If they do not see the prompt, the desired behavior will not happen. In other words, first and foremost, your prompt should attract attention.

The big challenge when designing a prompt is that multiple prompts are often fighting for the visitor's attention simultaneously. But you are the behavior designer. After reading this chapter, you will have smart techniques at your disposal, based on what psychology has taught you. We'll line them up for you, starting with motion, as that is the most powerful attention grabber.

Attracting attention with motion

- *Motion onset*
  The transition from static to moving attracts our attention big time. This sensitivity to motion onset is a deeply rooted survival mechanism. Try making your most important call-to-action button suddenly move from 'standstill'.

- *Looming motion*
  An object that is becoming bigger might be something threatening. This immediately catches our attention. Try zooming in with your banner, for example. Or let a button or image slowly grow slightly larger.

- *The illusion of movement*
  The illusion of movement also attracts more attention than a static picture. This is good to know, as sometimes you can't use movement in your online environment, because of brand guidelines, for example, or because it's technically too complicated. In such cases, use an image that shows movement, like a man in a running pose, a stone halfway through its fall or a car with three cartoon-like lines behind it, suggesting that the car is at full speed.

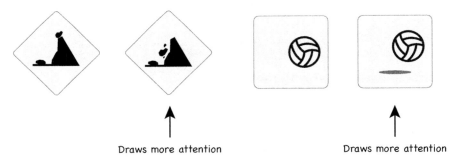

Attract attention with salience

- *Shapes and colors that stand out*
  It's an old jungle law: something that stands out is a potential threat or potential food. The psychological principle 'Salience' is based on this: the more your buttons, advertisements or other online prompts deviate from their visual environment, the more attention you will attract. For example, design your button in a color that contrasts with the background; this usually leads to more clicks. If you are designing a banner, try an oblique frame or round shapes, because most other banners are rectangular:

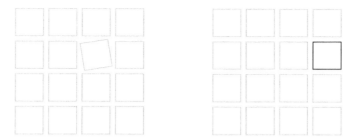

The badge app symbol has a different size, shape, and color than the app icon and only partially overlaps, which makes it look like it is separate. This attracts attention:

- *'Bizarre' messages*

A 'bizarre' message is also a form of deviation. In psychology, we call it the 'Bizarreness effect'. For example, use a (positive) word or image that does not fit with your organization or product at all. Or something absurd, like 'Nobody calls their kid Scooby Doo'. Please note: this requires creativity, guts, and a good feeling for how far you can push the boundaries. And it only works if you are known to the recipient as the sender, otherwise, you run the risk of coming across as unreliable. The following example comes from Obama's election campaign:

Bizarreness-effect
The president of the US addressing you with "Hey"

Attracting attention with people or animals

- *People and animals*
  Human shapes, animals, eyes, faces, silhouettes – they have always prompted our vigilance. When this happens, System 1 says to System 2: now you really have to pay attention because this will be fighting, fleeing, feeding or fornicating. It is a good reason to show a person on your product photos.

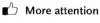 **More attention**
Images of people

 **Less attention**
Without images of people

- *Strong emotions*
  Strong emotions are extremely important from an evolutionary point of view: when we see someone who is super happy or screams with fear, we know something special is going on. We can use this principle if we want to attract attention. For example, use an image with strong emotions. Words that are associated with emotion also have higher click-through ratios than neutral words, according to analyses of millions of successful advertisements and headlines. In addition, negative emotions attract more attention than positive emotions, both in images and text. For negative emotions, do check carefully whether they suit your brand and your message.

More attention
With strong emotion

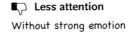 **Less attention**
Without strong emotion

Tip: use strong, negative emotions to attract attention, but be careful using them during the remainder of the customer journey. Persuasion is much easier when the atmosphere is friendly and pleasant.

Three-word phrases or trigrams that yielded the most Facebook engagements (likes, shares, comments) in 2017 in relative terms[9]

- tears of joy
- make you cry
- give you goosebumps
- is too cute
- shocked to see
- melt your heart
- can't stop laughing

You certainly don't have to apply these attention-grabbing principles all at the same time. Using one or two principles is often sufficient. Think about what best suits your brand and what fits well with the rest of the customer journey.

  Attract attention with something that moves, something that deviates, a person, an animal, or a strong emotion

What should you remember?

- If your prompt is not seen, it's 'game over' straight away.
- So a prompt only works if it attracts the most attention.

What can you do?

- Attract attention with something that moves, something that deviates, a person, an animal or a strong emotion.
- Try to use motion first, because that's the strongest attention grabber.

We can only focus on one thing at a time and do only one behavior

HOW TO DESIGN A WINNING PROMPT

Competing prompts

Say you're going to a party. You walk in and immediately fifty people start talking to you to get your attention. What do you do? You'll probably run away screaming. That's a crazy situation, you might think. But online, this happens all the time.

Many home pages and landing pages are full of prompts: buttons and links that invite us to click on them. 'Check out this offer, read more about us, log in, no wait, check the latest news, or no, get inspired here'. 'Don't forget to download the app! Make sure you subscribe to our newsletter, and in between:

can we get permission to send you a message?' 'And now quickly scroll down, because there's more, much more.'

This is a lot of work for our brain. We have to ignore all these competing prompts and concentrate on what we really want. From a behavior design perspective, this doesn't make any sense. There is a good chance that we will lose our visitors as a result. Or that they don't get around to doing the behavior we want.

Avoid competing prompts

We can only (really) focus on one thing and only show one (good) behavior at a time. This means that if you want to change a person's behavior, you will have to get their full attention. In an environment with multiple prompts, this means: eliminating prompts and designing the winning prompt, which leads to the behavior you want. Because remember: there is always a winning prompt.

In your own environment, you have a good grip on that. There, it's a matter of eliminating prompts. On your website, for example, you can determine for each page which behavior you would like the most from your visitors. Design a clear call to action that attracts attention to prompt this behavior.

There are probably also visitors who want something different than the behavior you want. Hide the links to these parts in a drop-down menu, for example, or give them less attention. If a visitor wants something specific – such as finding the opening hours – it doesn't matter that there is no prompt on the homepage for this. You can help this visitor with good navigation and a proper search function, too.

So why do people often put in so many different prompts? The idea is usually: something for everyone. One person is looking for inspiration, another to download a white paper, and yet another for the vacancies. Many websites have different goals, after all. The only way to address this is to direct the people you are addressing outside of your website to special landing pages, where you can really design a single route for each behavior.

The battle for the homepage

For larger organizations, designing the homepage, in particular, is a hassle. Different teams want to put their product or service in the spotlight in this 'shop window of the company'. But what can you do: space is limited.

One notorious false solution is the carousel. By changing the content on the homepage every few seconds, it seems like extra space is created. But from a behavior designer's point of view, this is utter madness. As if your visitors are going to watch a home page patiently, like a TV show. A/B tests show that these carousels lower the conversion rate in most cases. As a behavior designer, you can see why: the more prompts at once or in succession, the harder it is to find your way. System 2 then takes complete control, which means that the chance of leading someone into a certain direction is pretty much lost.

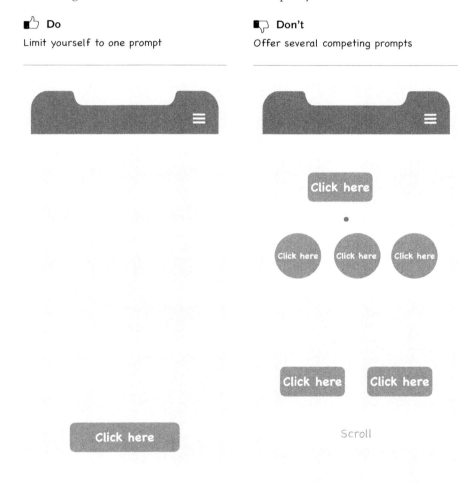

Of course, it's tricky to claim the homepage all to yourself and only show one prompt. One good strategy is to really promote one behavior with a clear prompt and to offer the rest of the prompts as a menu or a list. This will lead your visitors towards the right landing page, where you can implement the one-prompt strategy.

 Do

Choose one primary prompt, and give other prompts less emphasis.

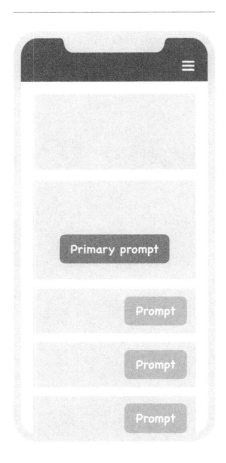

 Limit the number of prompts, preferably to one, or make the most important prompt stand out

What should you remember?

- We can only focus on one thing at a time.
- We can only do one behavior at a time.
- If there are too many competing prompts, we become 'paralyzed' and do nothing.

What can you do?

- Limit the number of prompts, preferably to one.
- If you have to offer several prompts, make the most important prompt stand out.

A good design makes us understand subconsciously and lightning-fast what we are able to do

HOW TO DESIGN A WINNING PROMPT
Affordance

You may recognize this: you want to walk into an unknown building, but you don't know whether to push or pull that door. That is not your fault, it's the designer of the door. They didn't consider the Affordance principle.

👍 **Good affordance**
The design of the door communicates wether you need to push or pull.

👎 **Bad affordance**
It feels like you need to pull, but the instruction says 'push'.

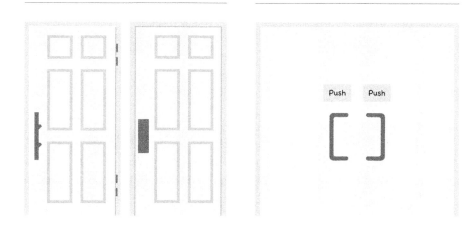

A door handle, a school bell, a baseball, a play button, a send button: you know immediately what to do with them when you come across them, in some cases even if you've never seen them before. American psychologist Donald Norman, known for his bestseller *The design of everyday things*, calls this 'affordance'.[10] We have defined this term as follows:

Affordance is the extent to which an object, with its forms and other properties, makes clear how it is operated.

Norman himself gives the example of a chair. The four legs, the flat surface, the ergonomically shaped horizontal bars, the balance between the various parts, possibly the proximity of a table: combined, they almost beg you to sit down on it. Our unconscious brain automatically and rapidly interprets the visual properties that communicate 'seatability', so that we do not have to consciously think about where we can sit down. This makes a chair an object with excellent affordance.

no affordance   affordance

Innate and learned

The lightning-fast and unconscious perception of affordances is often learned through interaction with our environment. For example, by using websites and apps we have learned which visual elements are clickable, what is scrollable, what we can close or open, and what we can expand or collapse.

But if you use a computer for the first time, you would find it difficult to navigate a website. How would you know that a text underlined in blue is clickable? There are also differences between cultures. For example, in China everybody knows that in the chat program WeChat, an icon with a red envelope can be clicked; you will then receive an amount of money. Here in the West, this is not evident (but luckily, now you know).

Online affordance

Pay close attention to affordance when designing a prompt as an online behavior designer. System 1 must understand at a glance what it should do with that prompt and how. Click! Scroll! Swipe! You don't want System 2 to have to think about what's clickable and what's not. Otherwise, you would be wasting valuable thinking time and making the desired behavior unnecessarily difficult.

But when you think like a behavior designer, you don't use your designing skills to design something unique, but to make something clear and functional. A few examples:

- Instead of a minimalist, square order button: an elongated 3D order button.

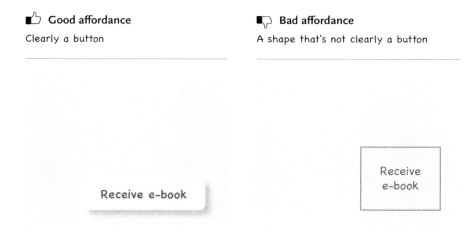

👍 **Good affordance**
Clearly a button

👎 **Bad affordance**
A shape that's not clearly a button

- Instead of artistic line play as an input field: a white area with drop shadow and a blinking cursor. An additional advantage is that a contrasting white surface and a blinking cursor attract attention.

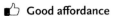 **Good affordance**
White background color, shadow and blinking cursor communicate that this is an input field without any doubt.

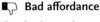 **Bad affordance**
Our brain needs more time to understand that this is an input field.

- Instead of a self-conceived shape button to start your video: the well known triangle, which has become popular for a reason.

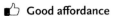 **Good affordance**
When we see a 'play' button, we immediately know what it means and how it works.

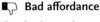 **Bad affordance**
In this example, it takes us longer to understand what we can do here.

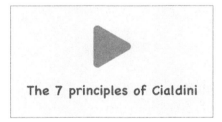

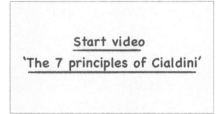

Scroll with it

Finally, a form of affordance that you need on almost every path of persuasion: scrolling. Too often, it is still not clear to visitors that they can scroll down, usually because there is a so-called 'false boundary' at the bottom of a piece of content. This means it seems that the page has stopped, while there is still persuasive information, just out of sight:

👍 **Good scrolling affordance**
Cutting off the background surface allows our subconscious brain to understand that the page continues.

👎 **Bad scrolling affordance**
It appears as if the page stops. We are not subconsciously encouraged to scroll.

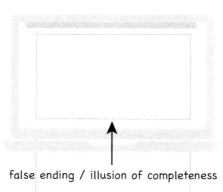

false ending / illusion of completeness

👍 **Good scrolling affordance**
Cutting off the image allows our subconscious brain to understand that we should continue to scroll.

Tip: if you feel the urge to add an instruction to explain how it works, the affordance is probably not good.

 Make it clear in a millisecond that your prompt is clickable

What should you remember?

- A good design makes us understand subconsciously and lightning fast how we can interact with it.
- We are often quicker to see what we have to do with something than to know what it is exactly.
- When this happens, the design has good affordance.
- A design with good affordance saves your visitors a lot of mental effort.
- Good affordance, therefore, leads to more people interacting with your prompt.

What can you do?

- Make it clear in a millisecond that your prompt is clickable.
- Give buttons an obvious button shape.
- Use commonly used shapes that most visitors won't even have to think about.
- When designing a prompt, your aim is not to win an originality award.

Behavior becomes easier when you tell people exactly what to do

HOW TO DESIGN A WINNING PROMPT

Name the desired behavior, literally

'Go brush your teeth, put on your pajamas, clean up your Legos, turn off the light, lie down in your bed.' Have you ever put a child to bed? Then you know that at a certain point, you start using the imperative to make them hurry along. You should actually do the same with your visitors online.

Ask for the desired behavior.

If we want someone to hurry up, we – unconsciously – name the desired behavior literally, in the imperative mode. In this way, we help the other person's brain to initiate the behavior. And so we make the behavior simpler. And the less unnecessary mental effort, the greater the chance of achieving the desired behavior.

Take a look at the following examples:

👍 Do
Use a verb in the imperative form as a prompt.

👎 Don't
Use a noun as a prompt.

Enter your details

Email address

[Type your email address here, i.e. john@example.com]

Tick your preference
- ☐ Daily updates
- ☐ Monthly offers
- ☐ Notice of changed opening times

Your details

Email address

[I.e. john@example.com]

Your preference
- ☐ Daily updates
- ☐ Monthly offers
- ☐ Notice of changed opening times

In the example on the left, we always use a clear and concrete verb. This increases the chance of conversion.

Ability

Prompts that tell you very clearly what to do work better than prompts that use more abstract terms. In the example on the left, we could also have used 'Indicate your preference here'. But 'Tick' is more concrete than 'Indicate' and, therefore, easier to follow up.

Click here or swipe up

When you want to encourage your visitors to click while they are busy doing something else, naming the physical behavior often works best. System 1 is more likely to understand physical actions like 'Click here' and 'Swipe up' than more abstract references like 'Discover the benefits' or 'Request a quote'.

Please note that a usability expert will probably argue against using 'Click here' because it is a well-known UX guideline that you should use a verb that represents the result of the desired behavior for your call to action, for example, 'Request the brochure'. While there is certainly something to be said for this in many places on your website, this is not the case if you need to divert your visitor away from another task. In that case, it's better to design a prompt that is fully focused on System 1.

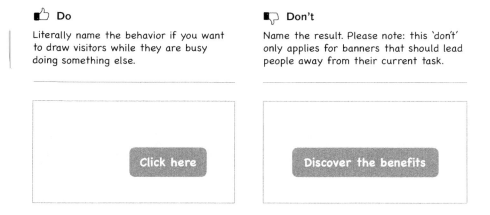

 Literally name the desired behavior, in the imperative

What should you remember?

- Behavior becomes easier when you tell someone exactly what to do.
- For verbs, the imperative ('Enter your name') works best.

What can you do?

- Literally name the desired behavior, using the imperative form.
- Feel free to use 'Click here' for a prompt that should divert your visitor from other behavior.

Curiosity leads us away from our path

HOW TO DESIGN A WINNING PROMPT
Curiosity

How amazing would it be if there were an almost bottomless bin? You would want to take a closer look, wouldn't you? They tried it in Sweden, and successfully so.

This experiment was part of the Fun Theory project. Volkswagen wanted to show that fun is the key to changing behavior. The researchers installed a special trash can in a city park. They mounted the necessary electronics on the inside, and on the outside they stuck the following text in large letters: *The world's deepest trash can*. Every time someone threw trash into the can, the cartoon-like sound of an object falling into an unfathomable depth was heard, obviously followed by a big thud after a few seconds. If you weren't encouraged by the text on the trash can, you certainly were by the surprised people who had gathered around it:

150 lbs.   65 lbs.

WORLD'S DEEPEST TRASH CAN

The researchers were right: fun is a determining factor in behavioral change. So it's not surprising that on a certain day the trash can collected 150 pounds of waste, as opposed to 65 pounds in a nearby can. But what was crucial in the experiment, was that the trash can first made people curious: why the deepest trash can in the world? And: why do the people around that trash can look so excited?

Shifting attention

Here's the lesson you can learn from this case as a behavior designer: with curiosity you can motivate your visitors to take the desired action. Especially when it comes to the first prompt of a new behavioral route. Curiosity has the stopping power needed to entice people to stop what they are doing at the time. Perfect for advertisements, in other words.

But it doesn't stop with simply arousing curiosity. In fact: that's when the real persuasion begins. However, you already have people's attention: the first click, the first small step in the right direction.

How to design curiosity

With the Curiosity principle, it should be clear to your visitors that their curiosity will be satisfied immediately after clicking or scrolling.

> So not: "Will you be the winner of one million?",
> But: 'This is how you can win a million dollars!'

If you click on the first prompt, you know that you still won't get the answer. 'Whatever,' says System 1; it is not curious. But if you click on the second prompt, you know that you will be given an answer: your curiosity will be satisfied, so you just click.

This how-to construction is one of the five best-known ways to arouse curiosity. We'll line them up for you:

Signal words

Signal words like 'this' and 'these' refer to something you will see after the click. That's why they work well as a title (inviting you to read a text), a subject line (inviting you to open an email) and in advertisements (inviting you to click):

- This picture shows you what the car looks like on the inside
- This is what working in the future looks like
- This is what customers say about us

THIS PRINCIPLE MAKES YOU EVEN MORE SUCCESSFUL
Buzzsumo researched which trigrams (groups of three words) generated the most engagement on Facebook.[11] For this purpose, they analyzed one hundred million Facebook posts. 'Will make you ...' tops the chart. A few variations:

- 6 hard truths that will make you a better person
- Pictures that will make you laugh out loud
- 24 pictures that will make you feel better about the world

Why does this work so well? The content is directly linked to how it will make you feel. This makes you optimally curious to view that content.

The who
We like to mirror ourselves to others and to judge or admire others. References to persons make us curious.

- This is what Tanya looked like after taking our course
- This is what the Jones family thought of our arrangement

The how or why
Some people get curious when you tell them that you can teach them something. With words like 'how' and 'why' you can encourage their curiosity.

- Why we only use 5 percent of our brainpower
- How to get five pots of tea out of a single teabag

Lists
Lists make us curious, probably partly because they promise that we can learn something new quickly and because we like to know who or what won first place. We are competitive creatures.

- These are the most common mistakes in marketing
  (It also helps here that we just love mistakes)
- Ten ways to improve your conversion rate
  (It also helps here that we just love a profit)

Going against general views or expectations

Being confronted with something that goes against what everyone else thinks makes us feel uncomfortable. So we like to go and investigate exactly what's going on.

- We've got breakfast all wrong
- Exercise makes you fat

Text and image

These examples arouse curiosity with text. But when we advertise, we communicate visually first and foremost. And because curiosity is mainly aroused by what we do not yet see, this is a tough one. Still, there are possibilities:

- (partially) covering objects;
- showing a small part of a product;
- showing someone who's reacting to a product;
- showing a sneak preview (video).

Arouse curiosity by showing only a small part of the product.

Do not disappoint

Be careful not to disappoint your visitors. You have to make it clear in advance that their curiosity will be satisfied. Not with the weak reward that most click bait has in store for you, but with something really worthwhile. Otherwise, curiosity may have done its job as a prompt, but your visitors will drop out and may never come back.

 Persuade your visitors to click by making them very curious for a moment

What should you remember?

- Curiosity leads us away from our path.
- This is certainly the case when we know that our curiosity is also going to be satisfied immediately.
- Curiosity then reinforces the motivation to at least take a look.
- We call this the 'Curiosity strategy'.
- As behavior designer, you can use it to design prompts.
- Curiosity is used to get people to take the first step. Once that's happened, the persuasion game really takes off.

What can you do?

- Persuade your visitors to clicking by making them very curious.
- Do so in the text with signal words, with who, how, or why, with lists or with something that goes against general views or expectations.
- Do so visually by partially covering an object, showing only a small part of a product, showing a reaction to a product, or giving a sneak preview.
- Immediately show that their curiosity will be satisfied as soon as the visitor shows the desired behavior.
- Make sure you really satisfy that curiosity, and don't disappoint.

We stop what we are doing if we expect to gain an exceptional benefit

HOW TO DESIGN A WINNING PROMPT

Exceptional benefit

Let's be honest: do you get excited about a free newsletter? Or a 5 percent discount? Most people don't. Spoiled as we are, we shrug our shoulders and move on. That is, until we get an offer that really surprises us. That's when we drop everything.

When we're online, we are busy doing all sorts of things. We focus on social media, watch a jazz tutorial on YouTube, or may be busy emailing for work. System 2 focuses on the task, while System 1 keeps watch. In other words: System 1 unknowingly scans the texts and images we come across online. Fortunately, System 1 can ignore most of it, but occasionally we are distracted by a very interesting offer. An offer we can't refuse, like:

- 80 percent discount on a TV
- $100 cash back
- Watch unlimited box sets for free for three months

Too good to be true! Let's check it out, anyway:

👍 **Do**
Communicate an exceptional benefit with a maximum of five words.

As a behavior designer, you can generate stopping power by communicating one of these exceptional benefits. In other words: you are literally stopping people doing what they are doing. Conditions apply, however, if you want this Exceptional-benefit strategy to work for you. We will discuss them below.

Make it truly exceptional
As we said earlier: a 5 percent discount is unlikely to whet System 1's appetite. You should offer a real opportunity: something that offers a unique and fundamental advantage. High discounts, cashback offers, and low prices (see the examples we mentioned earlier) work well. Also consider simple solutions for everyday problems:

- No more bags under your eyes
- Your Christmas tree decorated in less than a minute
- Lose weight sitting down.

Keep it simple
We should not overcomplicate that exceptional advantage as we are communicating with System 1, which we compared to a seven-year-old child earlier. So

stick to simple sentences and preferably use no more than five words. System 1 tends to completely ignore long rambling pieces of text. If you stick to that number of words, chances are that System 1 will automatically read your message and distract your visitors from what they are doing.

Also use a large font, otherwise, no one will bother reading it. System 1 is not that easy to persuade, after all. And finally, use images that support your claim and make it clear even faster.

 Trigger your visitors with an offer that seems too good to be true

What should you remember?

- We stop what we are doing if we expect to gain an exceptional benefit.
- We call this the 'Exceptional-benefit strategy'.

- **What can you do?**

- Trigger your visitors with an advantage that seems too good to be true.
- Formulate this advantage in simple words and sentences.
- Use a maximum of five words.
- Use a large font and a supporting image where possible.

We answer simple questions
by automatic reflex

HOW TO DESIGN A WINNING PROMPT

Simple question

1   You've probably been there: just as you sit down to dinner, the doorbell rings. There is a student at the door, boldly asking: "Good evening, sir. Do you like animals?" Of course you do. Before you know it, you're engaged in a conversation that ultimately leads to a request to donate.

This chapter is all about that first question. In reality, this is the prompt to start a conversation. This strategy – let's call it the 'Simple-question strategy'–is based on our natural reflex to respond. As children, our parents and teachers taught us to respond politely when we were asked a question. In fact: if we failed to answer, we usually got into trouble. With pop-quizzes and tests, we feel the sheer joy of giving the correct answer.

Simple question with answer buttons
We can also use this irresistible urge to answer questions online: by asking a simple close-ended question, preferably with two, three or possibly four an-

swer buttons (five becomes too complicated). This is what Joris and his team at Buyerminds did for bol.com (the largest Dutch online retailer) when he was optimizing the review flow. In short, we wanted more reviews. In this case, the prompt that was supposed to trigger the behavior 'review writing' was an email that customers received after buying a product. We experimented with two variants:

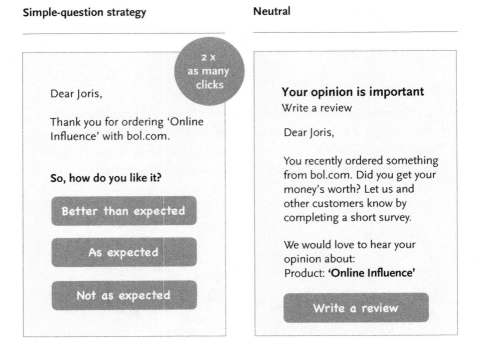

Please note:
This is a simplified version of the emails from the origional experiment.

It turned out to be effective: the left-hand variant – with the simple question and the three answer buttons – resulted in twice as many clicks. It was a great result, with which we jointly won the first Dutch CRO Award (for Conversion Rate Optimization).

The perfect pick-up line

A simple question is often a perfect opening line to start a customer journey. The main purpose of the question is to draw attention away from another activity. The real temptation process only begins after that. A few examples of simple questions:

👍 Simple-question strategy

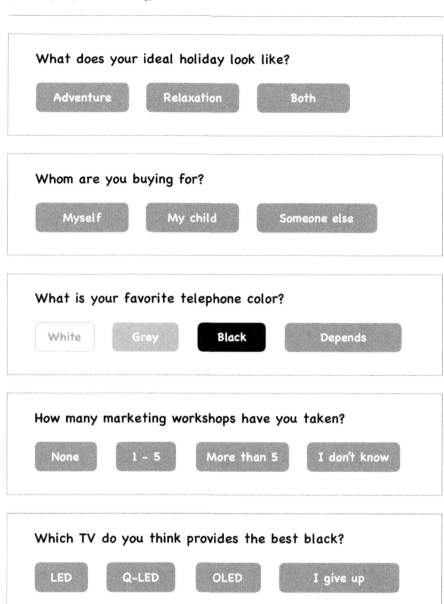

The latter is a pop-quiz question, because it does not ask for your personal preference. Questions like these are often irresistible.

Keep it simple
A tip: keep your question really simple, because you are using your prompt to address System 1, which you can compare to a seven-year-old child – as we

keep banging on about. A simple question is short, concrete, close-ended and easy to understand.

Keep it light

Your question should also be psychologically and socially 'safe'. In other words, answering the question should not make people feel like they are exposing themselves on a personal level or revealing private information. So keep it light:

 Don't
Ask a question that is too personal

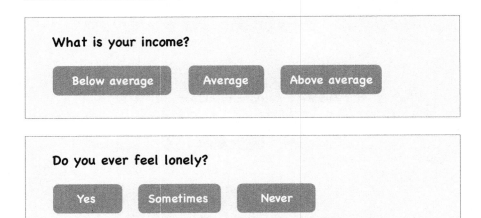

Always an answer

And finally: everyone should be able to answer the question. That means that you sometimes have to add options such as 'I don't know', 'Both' or 'Maybe'.

 Ask your visitors a question that is easy to understand and answer

What should you remember?

- We answer simple questions with an automatic reflex.
- We call this the 'Simple-question strategy'.

What can you do?

- Ask your visitors a question that is easy to understand and answer.
- Make sure your question is short, concrete, close-ended, and safe.
- Always offer choices: two, three or four.
- Make sure everyone can answer the question.

We do not like
unfinished business

HOW TO DESIGN A WINNING PROMPT
Unfinished journey

Maybe you are on LinkedIn, like many online professionals. The next time you accept a connection request, pay attention to the following. Instead of a page-filling confirmation or a thank-you, you will immediately see a prompt for a follow-up assignment.

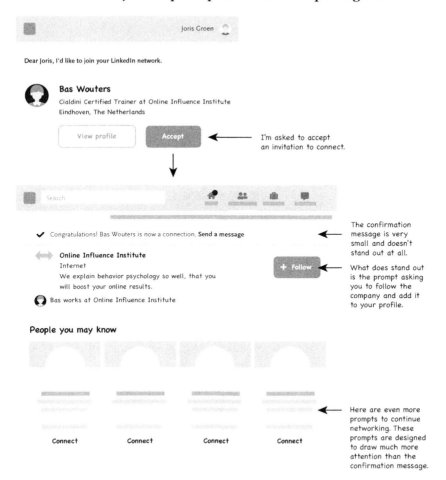

After the successful connection, you may have thought: right, and now back to work. But LinkedIn knows: now I have got you – and suggests that you complete your profile or make even more connections. With this prompt, the platform suggests that you're not quite 'done' yet. We call this the 'Unfinished-journey strategy':

The workings of this strategy are based on the following: we want to bring everything we do to a successful conclusion. Dropping out just like that makes us feel uncomfortable. As a behavior designer you can take advantage of this by looking for end stations, such as thank you and confirmation pages. That's where you ask for a new behavior. That only works if the new behavior is related to the last behavior. A few examples:

- In the thank-you email after registering for your online newsletter:
  Want to be completely up-to-date? Download our white paper

- After purchasing a plane ticket:
  Plan your trip to Schiphol immediately

- After choosing the currency in your travel app:
  Complete your personal profile

Immediately after I set the language to 'Dutch', I am prompted to create an account, so that I can add 'Dutch' to my personal settings.

The last step

Russian psychologist Bluma Zeigarnik discovered that unfinished tasks keep floating around in our brain.[12] It leaves us with a feeling of unease and motivates us to finish the task.

If you name the behavior as the last step needed to get a job done, you increase your visitor's motivation: come on, you're almost there, just one more click.

Airbnb does this very cleverly and does not ask you for a review after your trip, but encourages you with a clever line: "One last step to complete your journey." They apply Unfinished-journey strategy beautifully:

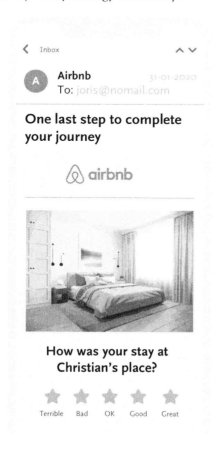

 Name the desired behavior as a logical next step

What should you remember?

- We do not like unfinished business.
- We are motivated by the idea that we are continuing a task or completing a journey.
- We call this the 'Unfinished-journey strategy'.
- Thanks to the Zeigarnik effect we are extra motivated to take the final step.

What can you do?

- Name the desired behavior as a logical next step.
- This works even better if it is the last step required to complete a customer journey.

Part 3

How to boost motivation

HOW TO BOOST MOTIVATION

What is motivation?

Now that you know what prompts are and how to use them to trigger your target group, in this part of the book we will discuss the second element of the Fogg Behavior Model: motivation.

We regularly use the word 'motivation' in everyday life. Just think how many times we say we're super-motivated. Or, conversely, that we are lacking motivation. Motivation is all about our inner drive to do something. It is based on a variety of factors: pleasure and pain, hopes and fears, and social acceptance and rejection. We will walk you through all six of them. Next, we will show you how to motivate your visitors towards the behavior you want to see.

Pleasure and pain

We want to feel good and avoid pain. This is the most primitive form of motivation; we also observe it in animals. These two factors are all about the here and now.

Simply relaxing in the sun is an example of our urge to feel good in the offline world. And sheltering from the rain is one way to try to avoid pain, or wet clothes. Spontaneously 'falling in love' with a beautiful image is an example of feeling good online. But we also enjoy a juicy gossip story or a challenging game. Although we don't really experience physical pain online, irritations can sometimes come very close. Imagine a website that suddenly plays a loud noise: we tend to click it shut. The same goes for pop-ups that get in our way on a page we want to read. Sometimes these irritations run so high that we are only too happy to pay for an online service to get rid of those annoying advertisements.

Hopes and fears

Hopes and fears are mainly about what we want to achieve in the long term. When we hope, we do not immediately experience pleasure from our behavior, but expect to be rewarded for it in the future. And when we experience fear, we expect it to lead to future pain or loss.

Hope and fear encourage us to think ahead. For example, we subscribe to a newsletter in the hope that it will eventually make us smarter. In contrast, fear can prevent us from doing a behavior. For example, we can decide to not buy a pair of shoes, because we are afraid that others won't like them.

The general rule is: the greater the anticipated reward, the more motivated we are to go for it. And we will try even harder if we think we will get that reward quickly. Websites that reward us directly, for example, with direct access or fast order delivery, motivate us to do cumbersome work, such as filling in lengthy web forms. There is a reason why BJ Fogg says that the most noble way of persuasion only uses motivation based on an anticipated, better future.

Social acceptance and rejection

A special type of hopes and fears that drives our behavior has to do with our social life. Much of our behavior is driven by our desire to belong to a certain group. Or, at least, not to be rejected. We diligently contribute to forums, for example, without being paid for it. And some of us go to great lengths to get a few more likes on social media.

Online apps eagerly use these social motivators to persuade us to spend our time there. Because spending too much time on social media is only useful for advertisers, we believe that, as a behavior designer, you should be careful when using this form of motivation. Therefore, make sure the behavior you are trying to entice is always in your visitors' best interests.

Focus on visitors who are already somewhat motivated

As mentioned earlier, of the three factors in the Fogg Behavior Model (motivation, ability and prompt), motivation is the most difficult to influence. A person's motivation to pursue a specific goal is not easy to create. The extent to which we want something depends, for example, on our experience, our social environment, and the media. However, our individual personality also determines what motivates us and what does not.

Take the urge to order a new iPhone, for example. It stems from the experience with your previous iPhone, the phones of the people around you, the limitations of your old iPhone and the wonderful promises on the website of the new iPhone. As an online behavior designer, you usually only influence the latter aspect. This means your role is limited.

This is why BJ Fogg strongly advises not to focus on visitors you still need to motivate, but on visitors who are already somewhat motivated. By designing effective prompts specifically for them and making the desired behavior simple, you optimize your chances of influencing. Or, as the man said himself:

> *"Put hot triggers in the path of motivated people."*

By 'hot triggers', he means prompts to which visitors can respond directly. In earlier versions of the behavior model, the word trigger was used instead of prompt.

Let's take a simple example to clarify what we mean. Suppose you were selling umbrellas: it's obviously best to offer them during a rain shower, preferably to people who came to the mall without an umbrella. Similarly, the quickest way to sell tickets to a football match is to send club fans and football fans a message with a link to the ticket shop one week before the match.

So, the art of persuasion is not about 'advertising' an umbrella or football tickets. It is about offering a prompt at the right time and making the desired behavior simple.

Giving motivation a little nudge

So, is there nothing you can do to increase the motivation of visitors? Sure there is. You can use online content to boost motivation at the time of the prompt. This may not necessarily create motivation, but it does awaken it. To succeed, there are some tried and tested tactics.

For example, football fans may not be sufficiently motivated to purchase tickets for a match. Maybe that's because the game is also shown on television. Or because it is very difficult to get to the stadium. In such cases, these people are below the action line in the Fogg Behavior Model. This means that they are not going to buy tickets.

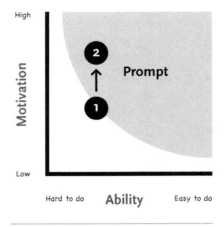

By giving motivation a little nudge, a larger proportion of your target group will end up above the action line.

As a behavior designer, you can apply multiple strategies to give them a nudge in the right direction. This increases the chances of conversion. For example, you can use social proof and say that many other fathers with children have bought tickets. Or you could use loss aversion and say that this might be the last chance to see a particular player in action live. Or you can create anticipatory enthusiasm and show pictures of happy spectators.[13]

In the following chapters, we will explain ten of these strategies. We start each chapter by briefly explaining the principle. Next, we substantiate our explanation with cases and online applications. And further on in this book, we will show you how to apply the principles in practice at the resource level. We will also tell you how we used them to help our customers.

Ten principles of motivation

1. **Anticipatory enthusiasm**
   Help your visitors anticipate by visualizing future rewards.

2. **Appealing to basic needs**
   Analyze which basic needs are related to your offer, and use words and images that refer to them.

3. **Social proof**
   Show clearly that others – preferably people who are similar to your visitors – also display the desired behavior.

4. **Authority**
   Show that you are an authority or borrow authority from others.

5. **Baby steps**
   Use baby steps to motivate your visitors step by step towards the desired 'main' behavior.

6. **Scarcity**
   Find out how you can make something even more attractive by emphasizing its scarcity, in terms of time or stock.

7. **Positive feedback**
   Be generous with compliments.

8. **Loss aversion**
   Frame the desired behavior as a way to prevent loss.

9. **Perceived value**
   Show how much effort you are putting in and let your visitors put effort into something.

10. **Reasons why**
    Find out what (good) reasons your visitors may have to show the behavior you want and state those reasons in your design.

Motivation boosters come at the expense of simplicity

However, there is a side note: trying to enhance motivation comes at the expense of simplicity and, therefore, ability. This is because our brain notices, reads and processes every piece of 'motivation-enhancing content'. In other words: every piece of that content that you add, costs us extra mental effort to process. Sometimes even so much that our ability to do the desired behavior decreases significantly.

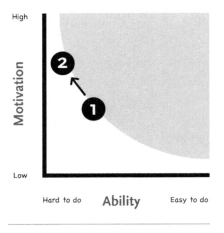

Motivation-enhancing content can reduce ability, thus undoing the positive effect on conversion, or even lowering it.

Novice behavior designers often get so excited about all the available strategies that they deck out their website with every persuasion principle they can think of. In practice, this is often counterproductive. Use this 'extra' content sparingly and carefully and try to find out which principles increase the motivation for your offer the most.

EXTRINSIC MOTIVATION

So far, we have talked about *intrinsic* motivation: motivation that comes from within. But sometimes, 'persuaders' also generate additional rewards. Take a five dollar discount, for example, if visitors sign up for a newsletter. In such cases, it is about *extrinsic* motivation: motivation that comes from the outside. Taking advantage of this can be clever if the intrinsic motivation is not strong enough. The extrinsic reward can serve as an initial push. In the case of the newsletter, the intrinsic motivation to read the newsletter can increase after reading the first newsletter. But the extrinsic five dollar reward was needed to make users motivated enough to subscribe.

Anticipating a future reward drives goal-directed behavior

HOW TO BOOST MOTIVATION

Anticipatory enthusiasm

You may have come across this: when a person who has taken a vacation enjoyed the anticipation even more than the vacation itself. Anticipation is a good example of how we can happily look forward to wonderful moments in the future. But here's the thing that's even more interesting for behavior designers: anticipation also plays a role in realizing goal-oriented behavior.

KLM increases anticipation with point-of-view photography of the future reward: a diving experience in Curaçao.

Dopamine motivates

Dopamine plays an important role in anticipating future rewards. Dopamine is a so-called neurotransmitter: a chemical element that plays an important role in communication between brain cells.

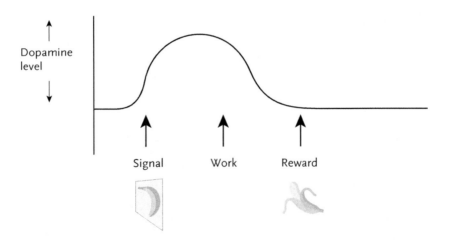

Psychologists used to assume that thanks to dopamine, we experienced happiness when *receiving* a reward, also known as 'liking'. This is because dopamine induces a pleasant feeling as soon as it is released into our brains. But new studies conducted with monkeys show that dopamine is mainly about *antici-*

pating a reward. In psychology, this is called 'wanting': the desire for a certain reward, which motivates you to take action[14].

The monkey experiment went as follows.[15] As soon as a signal went off, the monkey understood that a reward was on its way: a tasty drink. To get the drink, he had to do some 'work': repeatedly pressing a button. While the monkey was performing the task, more dopamine was measured in his brain than before. And when he received the reward, his dopamine level actually went down. In other words: the dopamine level mainly rose *prior* to the expected reward. This made the monkey feel better and become more active, stimulating him to realize the desired behavior.

UNCERTAIN REWARD? EVEN MORE PLEASURE.
The monkey experiment was also set up to find out to what extent the certainty of a reward influences our desire. The monkey only got a reward in half of the cases after pressing the button. The result: his dopamine level was twice as high. So, the pleasure increases even more with anticipation of a variable reward. It seems that nature makes us even more active in such cases with an extra shot of dopamine to find out how we can remove this uncertainty. Uncertain rewards can make us addicted to the large amount of dopamine that comes with chasing it. Take the casino, for example, where gambling is the 'work' and winning or not winning the uncertain reward.

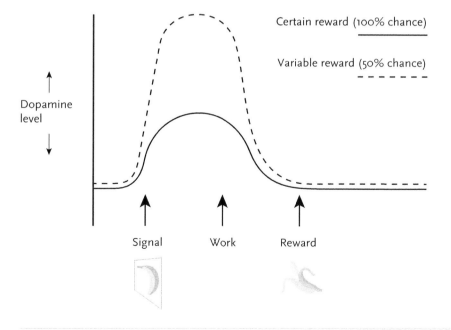

Facilitate anticipation ...

You can usually apply this principle fairly easily in your online environment by literally showing your visitors the potential reward. If a person is booking a beach vacation, for example, show them pictures or videos of a tropical island. If the final destination is New York, show them the skyline. Preferably photographed from the point of view of your visitor and realistic, so that the future moment of happiness can easily be anticipated. Of course, the greater the reward, the greater the desire. But also: the sooner you expect the reward, the stronger your desire for it. For example, it may be that imagining a small incentive that you receive immediately, such as a free beach ball when booking your holiday, releases as much dopamine as imagining the actual holiday, which is a lot further away in the future.

You can also use text to create an image of the future reward. If a person is about to book a hotel room, consider a sentence like: 'There's a delicious bottle of Prosecco with your name on it.' It might just be the decisive nudge towards an actual booking.

... throughout the customer journey

You may think: hold on, I'm already showing them the reward, right? After all, a professionally made website or app usually already has attractive images and clever texts. More often than not, you can look further, literally and figuratively. The trick is to boost the dopamine level not only at the start of the sales funnel but also throughout the rest of the funnel.

As an online behavior designer, you can, for example, show the chosen product – the future reward – on both the product page and every subsequent step. Your visitors will also produce dopamine during the final steps of the sales funnel and stay motivated to proceed to the next step.

👍 **Do**	👎 **Don't**
Show the future reward along with the order form.	A dry form.

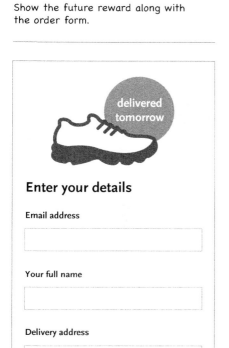

Inspiration for happy moments

There is an easy way to find the right dopamine-enhancing images for your visitors. Create a timeline and plot all your visitors' future happy moments. In the following scheme we have applied this to registering for a training:

Time →				
Happy moment	Acquiring access to the training	Completing the training	Passing the exam	Applying the knowledge successfully
Image	A screenshot of the learning environment	A screenshot of a full progress bar	A certificate	An image of applauding audience at a TED talk

The future reward that you show can, therefore, be more than the physical product that people will receive. You can also show the happy end-result of the product or service. Think of a wrinkle-free face after using a day cream, a trained body after visiting the gym and the applauding audience after that TED talk.

Concrete and simple

By the way, don't forget that anticipatory enthusiasm is a System 1 affair. In other words: use concrete images and stick to short and simple texts.

 Help your visitors to anticipate by visualizing future rewards

What should you remember?

- Imagining a future reward drives goal-directed behavior.
- Anticipation can be evoked by showing the future reward.
- Rewards that *immediately* follow the desired behavior have a greater effect.
- We call this the 'Anticipatory-enthusiasm principle'.

What can you do?

- Help your visitors anticipate by visualizing future rewards.
- To do this, identify all future moments of happiness that may follow from the desired behavior and visualize or describe the best of them.
- Show these visualizations not only at the beginning of the sales funnel, but until the final moment of conversion.

Our motivation is based on a limited number of basic needs

HOW TO INCREASE MOTIVATION

Appealing to basic needs

In the 1930s, Emanuel Haldeman-Julius became incredibly wealthy by selling his *Little Blue Books*, in which the American printed the literature of writers such as Shakespeare and Goethe on cheap paper and in huge quantities. He sold more than two hundred million booklets of five cents each, the price of a hamburger at the time. The price was right, but sales were also boosted because he had come up with a clever idea.

Haldeman-Julius soon noticed that some books sold better than others.[16] In order to sell more of the less popular copies, he decided to rewrite the titles:

Original title	Rewritten title
Ten O'Clock 2,000 copies sold	*What Art Should Mean to You* 9,000 copies sold
Fleece of Gold 6,000 copies sold	*Quest for a Blonde Mistress* 50,000 copies sold
Art of Controversy 300 copies sold	*How to Argue Logically* 30,000 copies sold
Casanova and his Loves 8,000 copies sold	*Casanova: History's Greatest Lover* 22,000 copies sold
Apothegems 2,000 copies sold	*Truth About The Mystery of Life* 9,000 copies sold

Universal needs

By experimenting with the book titles and looking at the sales figures, Haldeman-Julius discovered the secret of best-selling titles. They all contain words related to universal human needs.

Examples are *Enjoyment of life* and *Winning*. And the title *How to reason logically* suggests that readers can learn something that helps them do their job better and possibly even outsmart others. A title such as *The Truth about the Mystery of Life* makes readers feel that life will become more understandable after reading the book.

Eight basic needs

In his book *Ca$hvertising*, copywriter Drew Eric Whitman lists these eight basic human needs that you can use if you want to motivate your visitors:[17]

1. Enjoyment of life, life extension
2. Enjoyment of food and beverages
3. Freedom from fear, pain, and danger
4. Sexual companionship
5. Comfortable living conditions
6. To be superior, winning
7. Care and protection of loved ones
8. Social approval

The idea behind this list is simple: link your offer to the fulfillment of one of these eight basic needs. This automatically increases your visitors' motivation to accept your offer.

If you use certain words or images, your visitors unconsciously make associations with these basic needs. In Kahneman's terms, System 1: thinks: yes, I want that too. This creates a positive emotion, after which System 2 gets down to work with the details of the offer.

With words ...

A few simple words are often enough to make your visitors associate with one of their basic needs. Take a look at the examples below:

Neutral text	Text with a stronger association with one of the basic needs	Basic need
Stay informed about our offers	Be the first to know about our offers	Winning
Travel with proper insurance	Protect yourself and your family	Protecting your loved ones
Enjoy your sun vacation	Get the most out of your life	Enjoyment of life

... and with images

You can also use photos and videos to associate with those basic needs. Again, we'll give you three examples:

Product	Image associated with a basic need	Basic need
An insurance package	Images of a carefree family on holiday	Avoiding fear, pain and danger
An online marketing course	A person being applauded after giving a presentation about the subject	Social approval
A smart thermostat	A family on the couch in comfortable clothing	Living comfortably

Your offer may also fulfill several basic needs at the same time. The expertise you gain during an online marketing course, will win you social approval. You'll also get promoted faster, make more money, and enjoy life more.

It goes without saying that your offer should really fulfill the underlying need. For example, we think that depicting exercising, healthy-looking people to sell sugary drinks or e-cigarettes is ethically questionable.

 Analyze what basic needs are related to your offer and use words and images that refer to them

What should you remember?

- Our motivation can be traced back to a number of basic needs.
- By appealing to these basic needs, you increase the motivation to respond to your offer.

What can you do?

- Analyze which basic needs are related to your offer.
- Use words and images that refer to them.

When we are unsure, we are influenced by the behavior of the people around us

HOW TO BOOST MOTIVATION
Social proof

Do you recognize this situation? You see a pair of beautiful shoes on Instagram. You click on them to see how much they cost. Not a bad price. But then suddenly, doubt strikes. Who is this supplier? Can I trust them? Or am I the only fool on the planet who's even contemplating ordering something from them?

At that moment, you probably already started looking for 'social proof', unconsciously. Social proof means all the signs that point towards others – preferably many others – who have happily been ordering from this supplier for many years.

Copying the behavior of others is built into our system. Why is that? We are not sure about many things, although we would like to be. That is why we look at what others do and follow their example at uncertain times – if we do not fully trust that online shoe supplier.

Social proof worth £5.4 billion
One case underlining the effect of social proof is that of the UK tax authorities.[18] They sent payment reminders to citizens who failed to pay their taxes on time. They wrote a letter to encourage them to do so. The letter came in four variants:

- The first letter was the original 'threatening letter'. It stated that the recipient of the letter was liable to pay monetary interest, a fine and ultimately risked a visit to the judge if they did not pay. Of the recipients of this letter, 67.5 percent paid their taxes.

- In letter number 2, they wrote that nine out of ten people in the UK pay their taxes in time. The result: 72,5 percent of the recipients paid their taxes. Based on that one small change, they copied the behavior of others.

- Letter number 3 said that nine out of ten people *in the same postcode* pay their taxes on time. The result: 79 percent of the recipients paid their taxes.

- And letter number 4 stated that nine out of ten people *in the same city* pay their taxes on time. The result: 83 percent of the recipients paid their taxes:

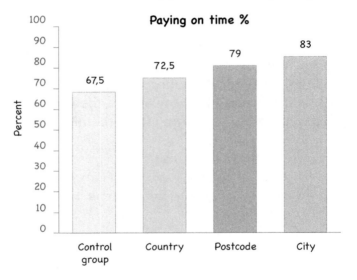

There are two things worth noting. First, that almost all recipients were sensitive to social proof: letter 2 convinced more people than letter 1. And secondly, the more the recipients could identify with the others, the greater the sensitivity: the difference between letter 4 and letters 2 and 3. Although the letter contained only minuscule changes, the effect was particularly significant. To this day, the British tax authorities have already collected an additional £5.4 billion in taxes with this one sentence.

The wisdom of the masses
The principle of Social Proof offers you plenty of opportunities to motivate your visitors to do the behavior you desire. In online environments too, we unconsciously allow ourselves to be guided by the wisdom of the masses. This is especially true when we have doubts about something or suffer from choice stress. In fact, Robert Cialdini calls social proof in an online environment his

most powerful persuasion principle.[19] Just think about how often you scroll through the reviews first when you make a purchase or reservation.

It makes sense, of course. When we buy online, we have nothing tangible to measure the product or service against. As a result, we ask ourselves all sorts of questions, even more so than we already do offline. Will it work as well as promised? Does it indeed offer the promised advantages? And is it really the best solution for my problem? In such situations, other people's opinions often give us the confidence we need to make a decision.

Booking.com

If there's one company that has turned the use of social proof into an art form, it's Booking.com. On its website, the booking company tells its visitors in all sorts of places, during the entire customer journey, what others have done or are doing. A few examples:

- You can see how many people are visiting the same page at the same time.
- You can see how many times a property has already been reviewed.
- You can see how many people have booked a property in the last 24 hours.
- You can see the average hotel visitor rating for this room or property.
- You can read reviews by people who have booked the property before.
- You can see from the large number of reviews that many people have already booked the property.
- You can see that certain properties have been awarded the 'bestseller' label.

In short, you are continuously getting confirmation that you are doing a great job: all these other people did or are doing exactly the same.

Three boosters

The great thing is: you can enhance the effect of social proof. Here are three ways to do so.

Booster 1: literally name the desired behavior

You can apply the first amplifier in any situation: literally naming the desired behavior. Basically, just as we described in the *Prompts* section. A few examples:

- Ten people who bought this product *have already given their opinion*.
- Twenty visitors *have already booked a training* with us today.
- 160 customers *have subscribed to* our newsletter.

This often works better than the more general "160 people preceded you."

Booster 2: people who look like us
Someone else's opinion is strong. The opinion of many others is even stronger. But the opinion of many others with whom we identify is the most powerful. That is why it is important to show social proof by people who look like your visitors, as with the letter from the British tax authorities. Some examples in order of specificness:

- Ten *entrepreneurs* who bought this product have already given their opinion.
- *20 entrepreneurs from Amsterdam have booked a training with us today.*
- *160 innovative entrepreneurs from Amsterdam have signed up for our newsletter.*

Booster 3: credibility
The third way to boost your social proof is credibility. To put it simply: the evidence should not feel like advertising. Booking.com does this well by mapping in real-time that someone has just booked a hotel room, including their country of origin and the time of arrival. This is how the site's behavior designers show that the data comes straight from their database and was not conceived in advance by a smart online marketer. The same goes for the numbers: don't give a made-up round number, but a real number. A few examples:

- *Eleven* entrepreneurs who bought this product have already given their opinion.
- *27* entrepreneurs from Amsterdam have booked a training with us today.
- *169* innovative entrepreneurs from Amsterdam have signed up for our newsletter.

Collecting social proof

If you want to harness the power of social proof in your online environment, you will need to collect it first. A few examples to get you started:

- Ask customers repeatedly for a review or testimonial.
- Let people respond to your content, for example with likes.
- Install analysis software to collect usage statistics.

HOW TO USE THE POWER OF REVIEWS

In online environments, reviews are the most important form of social proof. But how do you make the most of the power of reviews? We have investigated this question at a major seller of kitchen appliances. Our most striking findings:

- Have at least twenty credible reviews, preferably from people with whom your visitors can identify. If you have less than five reviews, your visitors will be inclined to think that acquaintances of the owner left reviews on his request.
- Also show the negative reviews. After all, social proof is all about trust and credibility. That's why visitors also like to see the less positive reviews. As a seasoned expert in persuasion, it goes without saying that you do not call those reviews 'negative', but frame them as 'critical': a negative review may just as well be the result of an overly critical customer. So allow your visitors to decide for themselves whether something is negative.
- Make it clear that everyone can review. For example, add a button: 'Write your own review'. This reinforces the impression that the reviews were actually written by other customers.
- In addition to ratings, also show human expressions. Good reviews include a rating, such as stars, in combination with a conversational term, as in this diagram:

    | 1 star | 'Very poor' |
    | 2 stars | 'Not so good' |
    | 3 stars | 'Good' |
    | 4 stars | 'Great' |
    | 5 stars | 'Exceptional' |

Example of a review overview that comes across as trustworthy: a rating in conversational language, an example quote, the number of reviews including the number of critical reviews, and a button that makes it clear that all customers can write a review.

Show social proof

Once collected, it's important that you show the social proof. That may sound logical, but too often we see that the reviews have been collected, but not shown or not in the right place. For example, we have managed to make a major difference for one of our clients by moving a number of reviews and the average rating to their homepage. Your visitors never deliberately scour your website or app for evidence. So, it's up to you to get it ready for them.

 Clearly show that others – preferably people who look like your visitors – also do the desired behavior

NEW BEHAVIOR? SOCIAL PROOF!
Social proof is extra strong if you ask people to do something they have never done before, like buying something they have never bought before. Or registering for something when they do not know the underlying organization well. At times like these, social proof is very effective, because it builds trust. That is why the principle works best at the start of your customer journey. Maybe not straight away in an advertisement, but at the top of your landing page or on your homepage. Proving that others are behaving in the same way or have done so before makes your visitors feel that they are not alone and gives them more confidence to decide.

What should you remember?

- In case of uncertainty, we heavily rely on others to determine our behavior.
- We prefer to follow people with whom we can identify.
- We call this the 'Social Proof Principle'.

What can you do?

- Show clearly that others – preferably people who look like your visitors – also display the desired behavior.
- Name the desired behavior, literally.
- Present your social proof credibly, clearly and especially at the start of your customer journey.
- Provide at least twenty credible reviews.
- Also show the critical reviews.
- Make it clear that everyone can review.
- In addition to ratings, also show human expressions.

We like to trust people
and parties who have more
expertise than we do

HOW TO BOOST MOTIVATION

Authority

Petco is an American retail chain that mainly sells pet products. In order to persuade more visitors to make a purchase, the company did something seemingly small: it gave its quality and safety logo a more prominent place on the homepage. Just a handful of pixels in a different location, you might say. But it made a huge difference.

Until then, that quality and safety logo had had a discreet place: in the bottom right corner of the homepage. By placing it at the top, right below the search field and in the direct field of view of the visitors, the number of conversions on the website increased by almost 9 percent. In terms of design, it was just a minor change for the listed Petco, but the result was a gigantic increase in revenue.

👍 **More conversion**
Thanks to showing a trustworthy authority, in this case, McAfee

👎 **Less conversion**
Without an additional authority

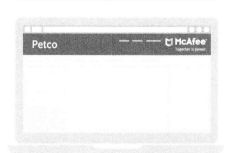

Connecting phone calls cleverly

A similar offline example comes from the practice of Robert Cialdini.[20] After a morning of observing a British real estate agency, the persuasion expert came up with advice that was as simple as it was effective for generating more client appointments: connect more cleverly.

Cialdini advised receptionist Sally to carefully introduce her colleagues to the caller from now on. If a person called with a question about commercial real estate, from now on she would say: "You have a question about commercial real estate? I'll put you through to Peter. He has twenty years of experience and is the go-to expert in this region." She did the same with Sandra if someone wanted to know more about private homes. Sally wasn't lying: Peter had indeed been in the business for twenty years and he really was an expert. And Sandra knew an awful lot about private homes.

The result? By introducing her colleagues as an authority, the receptionist increased the number of appointments by 20 percent. All the agreements together generated a 15 percent rise in signed contracts.

Get rid of that insecurity

Both Petco and Cialdini achieved success by using the Authority Principle. This principle appeals to our strong tendency to be guided by people we see as experts, or by symbols and signals that radiate expertise. They give us the feeling of certainty that we are looking for at times when we do not understand something properly or cannot assess it.

We do not always have the motivation or the opportunity to acquire the required knowledge or skills for something. For example, if you are looking for a new car as a layperson, it is difficult to find out which one has the best drive technology. In other cases, this possibility may be within reach, but we do not think it is worth the effort or the time investment. In such cases, isn't it wonderful to be offered the necessary authority on a silver platter? "Ah, Car of the Year. That probably means the drive technology is just fine."

Personal authority and 'borrowed' authority

There are two types of authority that you can use in your online environment: personal authority and 'borrowed' authority. By personal authority, we mean that you owe it to your own merits. A few examples:

- the training you have completed;
- the quality criteria that your products meet;
- the blogs or books you have written.

'Borrowed' authority is about the authority of others who are linked to you and, therefore, reflect positively on you. A few examples:

- the well-known clients for whom you work;
- the (fancy) office you're renting;
- the reviews by authorities in your industry.

Generating trust

For a crowdfunding company that is now well known, we once focused strongly on authority. It was a start-up at the time, with relatively little authority of its own. That's why we made use of borrowed authority on the website. To do so, we showed the logos of the Ministry of Economic Affairs, from which the company had received a subsidy, and of a well-known bank, which had invested in the company. The effect was clear: combined with a few other principles, this resulted in six times more revenue via the website.

Authority was particularly important for this start-up: a crowdfunding company is all about investing money, whereby trust plays a major role.

Not too modest

Research shows that we are all sensitive to such signals, consciously or unconsciously. So show the visitors of your online environment that:

- you are an authority in your field;
- you are connected to parties that have authority.

Don't be too modest. By showing your authority, you help your visitors. You save them the time it would take them to find out that you are indeed the right party. Because you can bet your bottom dollar that the clients of the British real estate agency were happy that they had found a wonderful expert like Peter or Sandra.

 Show that you are an authority and let others grant you their authority

What should you remember?

- We like to trust people and parties who have more expertise than we do.
- This tendency increases when we don't know the sender of a message too well.
- Not only people and parties can radiate authority, but also symbols and signals.
- We call this the 'Authority Principle'.

What can you do?

- Show that you are an authority.
- Let others grant you their authority.
- Don't be too modest.

We easily say yes to a small request and like to act in consistency with our previous actions and positions

HOW TO BOOST MOTIVATION

Baby steps

Would you be happy to place a huge billboard in your garden? Even if it is for a good cause? Almost three-quarters of homeowners in an American residential area were perfectly fine with it. Simply because they had just said yes to a question that seems harmless.

We are talking about the billboard research by Jonathan Freedman and Scott Fraser, a research that we also see in the work of Fogg and Cialdini.[21] The two social psychologists demonstrated that we like to act in consistency with our previous actions and points of view.

From a small request ...
In their first round of the residential area, they asked homeowners to stick a credit card-sized sticker on their window. The message on the sticker was: "Drive carefully!". They suggested it would reduce the number of accidents in the neighborhood. Most homeowners agreed to this request.

... to significant commitment
A few weeks later, the researchers continued their research. During this second round, they asked the same homeowners if they were happy to put a meter-high billboard with the same message in their front yard. 76 percent of the residents agreed. This was a significant percentage, given the control group of the research. The residents in that group were asked to put up the billboard immediately, without the prior request to place the sticker. Only 17 percent of them were happy to put up the large sign in their front yard;

Do
Ask for a small commitment first.

 Don't
Ask for a major commitment straight away.

So, what happened here? The homeowners who agreed to putting the sign in their garden had been guided by their tendency to act consistently with their previous behavior: placing the window sticker. BJ Fogg refers to that intermediate step with the sticker as a baby step. In other words: a small step that you get someone to take consciously, to make a larger step bridgeable. We like to act in consistency with our previous actions and positions, after all. As a behavior designer, you can make use of this if you want to encourage people to adopt certain behavior.

From big to small

Baby steps are generally very suitable for use in an online environment. Analyze where your visitors need to take a big step, such as downloading a white paper, buying a product or signing up for your training course. By paving the way with small steps, your visitors' commitment is likely to grow and the chance that they will eventually take that big step increases.

Let's make this concrete based on a case from our own practice. This case was about a job vacancy platform that allowed people to apply via a video message. As a first step, job seekers who clicked on an online vacancy had to download an app with which they could record their application:

Ask for a small commitment first

In other words: two very big steps. That's why we added several baby steps to the customer journey:

1. From now on, applicants had to fill in a form first, in which they could explain why they were suitable for the job. Compare filling in the form with placing the window sticker.

2. The following day, the applicants were sent an email with the following message: 'Congratulations! You are through to the next round.'

3. This was followed by downloading the app.

4. Next, we did not ask the applicants to get straight in front of the camera, because we felt a few minor commitments were needed first. That's why we gave them some job application tips first. We also told them the best way to record a video.

5. Only after the applicants had gone through all those baby steps could they really apply for the job by recording their video.

The creators of the app initially feared that with this approach it would take us too long to make our actual request: to record the video. The higher the number of steps, the lower the conversion, they thought. However, the number of clicks matters less than the size of the requested commitment. This turned out to be true: the number of video applications increased by 25 percent thanks to the addition of the baby steps:

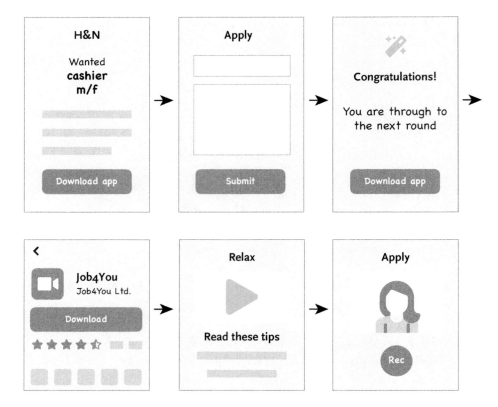

First, the safe steps

The case above was a fairly extensive customer journey. You can also use this Baby Steps principle on a smaller scale. Take the design of a form, for example. Most visitors do not like to enter their telephone number straight away. But if you start by asking for relatively 'safe' information, such as a person's product preference or preferred delivery method, the step of giving that phone number becomes a little bit easier.

First month free

Just look at how online services like Netflix and Amazon Prime incorporate baby steps. They often offer the first month for free. It's just a small step, because you can cancel after that month. But in many cases, it is a baby step that (partly) ensures that you ultimately become a paid member. For service providers in particular, this is one way to apply the Baby Steps principle fairly easily.

CELEBRATE EVERY BABY STEP
The following applies in behavior design: celebrate each baby step, for example, with a thumbs up or a different digital pat on the back. You can read more about this principle in the *Positive feedback* chapter further on in this part. A mini party after every baby step makes your visitors feel like they are making progress. This fits in perfectly with one of the basic principles of the Fogg Behavior Model: help people to feel successful.

Soft calls to action

In our case with the video applications, we used intermediate steps to guide the visitors towards a big step. However, you can also make a big step *sound* smaller. Online copywriters do this by choosing a 'softer' formulation for their calls to action. Compare the button texts below:

Soft CTA	**Hard CTA**
Feels like a small step	Feels like a big step
Compose your subscription	Subscribe now
Decide how much you want to donate	Donate

With the calls to action on the left, people feel that they are in control. In this way, we may not make the step smaller literally, but psychologically, it produces a different feeling.

Many roads

Finally, this observation: not all visitors need baby steps to proceed with the desired behavior. Some visitors are simply already convinced and want to take immediate action. It goes without saying that you do not want to slow them down. An additional 'Order now' button is a great solution in such cases. Or you could choose a single button if space is limited, with a combined call to action: 'Compose and order.' Either way, pave the way to the final destination with the right steps.

Use baby steps to motivate your visitors step by step towards the desired 'big' behavior

What should you remember?

- We easily say yes to a small request.
- We like to act consistently with our previous actions and positions.
- If you add small steps (baby steps) to the customer journey, you ultimately motivate your visitors to take a big step that they are more unlikely to take in one go.
- For every big step you can easily think up several smaller steps.
- Soft calls to action give people the pleasant feeling that they can always 'go back'.
- This is what we call the 'Baby Steps principle'.

What can you do?

- Use baby steps to motivate your visitors step by step towards the desired 'big' behavior.
- Ask yourself what the smallest, first step is that they must take to achieve the desired end behavior.
- Determine whether you can use that small first step for your call to action.
- Design a soft call to action for your button text to encourage click-through.
- Offer visitors who want to perform the desired behavior immediately an (additional) call to action.

We decide more quickly when time or stock is limited

HOW TO BOOST MOTIVATION
Scarcity

"We have to go on a date soon, because I'll be kicked out of university in three days": this is the romantic opening line that Facebook founder Mark Zuckerberg used to ask his wife Priscilla out. He scored big time with these words, because the two went on a date and got married a few years later. It just goes to show what the application of persuasion principles can lead to.

With his one-liner, Zuckerberg shifted the question from 'Do you want to?' to 'Is it still possible?' He probably didn't do it on purpose, but in doing so he made use of the Scarcity principle. We can summarize this principle as follows: our motivation to have something increases strongly if that something has limited availability, either in terms of time or stock.

(Online) sellers like to use this principle to motivate their visitors to take action. Think of slogans like: 'While stocks last', 'Only two places left' and 'Only today!' They all emphasize the limited availability of a product in terms of time and/or in stock. We will first discuss both strategies, followed by the combination of the two.

Scarcity of time
When there is scarcity of time, you increase the motivation to take action because there is a deadline: you only have so many days, hours or even minutes. A well-known example is the temporary offer, for example with an online discount code: 'Your time starts now. Only 23:59 hours left to redeem your discount!' Platforms such as Groupon, skyauction.com and websites offering cheap day outings have turned scarcity of time into a revenue model: you only have limited time to respond to an 'incredible opportunity'.

If you want to emphasize time scarcity in your own online environment, show your visitors a countdown timer. Don't make it too heavily animated, or it will start to feel like advertising.

Loud:

- Now or never!
- Last chance!
- When it's gone, it's gone!

Factual and more modest:

- Still 12 seats available
- Promotion ends in 02:03:33
- While stocks last

Scarcity in stock

In case of scarcity in stock, you increase motivation by making it clear that postponement can lead to something simply not being available in the future. So, your visitors need to take action, this minute. You often see this application of the scarcity principle on websites where you can book something: 'Last tickets!'

If you want to apply scarcity in stock yourself, think of a stock indicator that counts down from, say, five pieces to zero. Keep that indicator neutral so it doesn't come across as too pushy.

Only 5 in stock

Good to know: scarcity in stock usually has a stronger effect than scarcity in time. With scarcity in stock you do not know how long you have left to snap it up, because once it's gone, it's gone. Whereas with scarcity of time, you know exactly how much time you have left to take action.

Scarcity in time and stock

For the perfect application of the Scarcity principle, simply combine both forms of scarcity. Early-bird tickets for festivals are a good example of this. They are often available in limited amounts ('Only 500 tickets') and only for a certain period ('Until 21 April'). This generates optimal motivation to make the decision now and not to wait until it is too late.

Online ticket seller ViaGoGo takes this pretty far. On their website, they show exactly how many tickets are still available, including a message that there is a chance that they have already been sold in the meantime. If you want to score the tickets, you have to queue first. Once in the queue, you are asked if you really want the tickets, because otherwise they will go to someone else. And if you answer yes to that question, you'll be told you only have five minutes to buy them. This is how, step by step, they convert the question 'Do I really want those tickets for that amount?' into 'Will I be able to get my hands on them in time?'

Scarcity is always there

You may think that your products or services are not at all scarce and that as a result, you can't use the Scarcity principle. If that is the case, highlight what makes your product unique. Things that are unique, are scarce by default. Think of: ' The only protective cream that has not been tested on animals.' Or: ' The only online design course with a money-back guarantee.'

Also ask yourself what might happen to your visitors if they don't have your product. For a cream this might be: 'The longer you wait to protect your skin, the harder it will be to look younger.' And for travel insurance: 'The longer you travel uninsured, the greater the chance of a theft that won't be reimbursed.' These are also forms of scarcity. Make them explicit to increase the chance that your visitors will take action faster.

Be ethically responsible

Finally, a remark on ethics. The Scarcity principle is perhaps the most abused principle. You've seen it: the website says that there are only two seats left, but when you get there, the theater is almost empty. We can't be clear enough about this: don't do it. First of all, because it's unethical. Secondly, because it will ultimately work against you. People will find out, and who would come back to a company that fools its customers?

 Consider how you can make something even more attractive by emphasizing its scarcity, in terms of time or stock

What should you remember?

- We tend to decide faster if time is limited or stock is shrinking.
- We assign more value to things when they are scarce in terms of time and stock.
- We call this the 'Scarcity principle'.

What can you do?

- Consider how you can make something even more attractive by emphasizing its scarcity, in terms of time or stock.
- Ask yourself: is there scarcity of time? If so, consider how you can communicate that scarcity in a neutral way.
- Ask yourself: is there scarcity in stock? If so, consider how you can communicate this scarcity in a non-commercial way.
- An alternative way to apply the Scarcity principle is to highlight what is unique about your product, service or company.
- See if you can create scarcity by setting a deadline, for example in the form of a temporary promotion or a limited number of promotional items, such as early-bird tickets.
- Finally, you could ask yourself: what could go wrong if your visitors do not use your product or service?

We are motivated by pat on the back and compliments

HOW TO BOOST MOTIVATION
Positive feedback

It's Saturday night. After a busy week, you hit the town with your friends to celebrate life. The club is packed with fun people and the DJ is playing the best records. And then, at the climax of that huge hit song, suddenly it's raining confetti in the brightest colors. Is your response lukewarm? Or are you dancing even harder?

The latter, right? You were already in your element, but the colorful confetti shower reinforced your positive emotions. As a result, you become even more active than you already were, just like everybody else on the dance floor.

Why is it that we are stimulated by a handful of confetti? Or by a pat on the back, a compliment or applause? To find out more, we have included a study of patients with a rare brain disorder.[22] It shows that people whose frontal brain has been damaged no longer feel emotions. As a result, they are continuously in a kind of 'neutral' state in which they are no longer motivated to make decisions. They can still compare, reason and list the pros and cons, but they can't make decisions anymore.

In other words: feeling emotions is crucial when making decisions. And that is exactly what you, as a behavior designer, want to encourage your visitors to do. So, you would do well to treat your visitors to the necessary emotions during the customer journey.

Create positive experiences
Good to know: every environment evokes emotions, from fear and sadness to surprise and joy. Online environments are no exception. This is why the emotions we experience when we visit a website or use an app also influence our decisions and behavior. As a behavior designer, you can guide these emotions.

Research shows that visitors who have positive experiences during their customer journey are more likely to display the desired behavior than visitors who do not experience such emotions. A simple way to achieve this is to treat your visitors to a confetti shower. You guessed it: just like in that club on Saturday night. By continuously giving your visitors positive feedback during their customer journey, you awaken and maintain their positive emotions.

Every step is a party
Online environments offer countless opportunities to give people pats on the back and compliments. A well-known example is the green check mark when correctly completing a field in an online form. But there are more ways to give positive feedback. From complimenting phrases such as 'Well done' and a thumbs up, to dancing shopping carts. Allow your creativity to run wild:

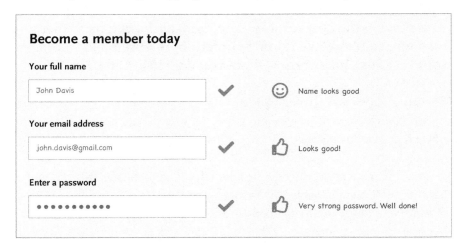

Good to remember: it doesn't matter how big or small the behavior is that you reward. As long as you're rewarding. Together, all these pats on the back make for a positive experience.

OVER THE TOP? NOT AT ALL
Behavior designers in countries where people are less generous with compliments, such as the Netherlands and Belgium, sometimes aren't keen on the idea of positive feedback. They think it's over the top and often state that visitors will understand immediately that the compliment is computer-generated. But that doesn't matter. BJ Fogg demonstrated that compliments that are clearly generated by a computer result in a more positive user experience.[23] Why is that? System 1, responsible for 95 percent of our decisions, is already blushing long before System 2 even realizes that a compliment is not genuine. In other words: keep the compliments coming.

Throw a party

If you want to motivate your visitors with a confetti shower, be sure to be generous with your confetti. Start by dividing the customer journey into chunks. Next, come up with big and small compliments that you can hand out during these steps. By doing so consistently, you keep stirring up positive emotions. This increases the chance that your visitors will complete their customer journey.

 Be generous with positive feedback

What should you remember?

- We are motivated by positive feedback and compliments.
- Without emotions, we would continuously find ourselves in a 'neutral' state in which we do not make decisions.
- Online, there are many opportunities to stir up and maintain positive emotions.
- Every step of the customer journey – big or small – is a potential party.
- We call this the 'Positive Feedback Principle'.

What can you do?

- Be generous with positive feedback.
- Provide positive feedback at every step of the customer journey.

We are twice as motivated to avoid loss than we are to gain the same thing

HOW TO BOOST MOTIVATION
Loss aversion

Imagine you are living in the Stone Age. You live in a cave, where you keep all your belongings. This means that every morning, you have to make a decision. Are you going to go out to collect new stuff? Or do you stay in the cave to guard your current possessions? You decide.

Because of evolution, people (and animals) experience loss as more intense than profit. That is why our ancestors generally 'chose' to cherish what they already had. They found the pain of loss as a result of looting more unpleasant than the prospect of new possessions.

Daniel Kahneman, among others, showed that it always stayed this way in the ages that followed.[24] His research showed that we are twice as afraid of losing something as we are attracted to get it. In psychology, we call this the 'Loss Aversion principle'. So, to increase your visitors' motivation, it can be a good idea to emphasize what they can lose instead of what can be won:

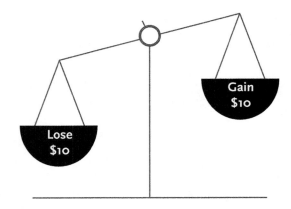

From profitable to loss avoidance

You can often very easily apply this principle in your online environment. Consider these two sentences:

- If you insulate your home fully, you'll be able to save 50 cents a day, every day.
- If you fail to insulate your home fully, you'll lose 50 cents a day.

The first sentence clearly emphasizes that you can 'win' something. The second sentence means exactly the same, but emphasizes what you can 'lose'. As it turned out, the latter had a lot more impact, because it led 150 percent more conversion.[25]

In the example below, two advertisements for breast cancer screening were compared[26]:

Communicate loss

125% more appointments

Breast cancer screening

Only 15% of Women Live 5+ Years with Late Detection. Get Screened.

medicalscreening.org

Communicate profit

Fewer appointments

Breast cancer screening

With Early Detection, Survival Rate is 100%. Book an Appointment today.

medicalscreening.org

The notice on the right focuses on profit: screening for survival. The notice on the left focuses on loss: screening to prevent you from dying. The notice on the left, which applied loss aversion, yielded 125 percent more appointments.

In another experiment, we tried to convince people who wanted to cancel their subscription to a service not to do so. We deployed different persuasion strategies using a chatbot. We were able to measure on the basis of which argument people clicked on the 'Yes, I will stay' button. The four arguments:

1   If you cancel, you will no longer enjoy the benefits of our product.
2   If you cancel, you will lose your loyalty points.
3   If you cancel, you will no longer support our charities.
4   Now is not the best time to cancel, because new features are coming.

The result? The vast majority of customers who continued their membership did so because they would otherwise lose their loyalty points (reason 2). In other words, the aversion to losing something was the decisive argument for them.

 Frame the desired behavior as the prevention of loss

LOSS AVERSION AND SCARCITY

The Scarcity principle we discussed earlier is, in fact, also about loss aversion. After all, scarcity is limited availability of something in terms of time or stock. This limited availability motivates us to take action earlier, because we are afraid of missing out.

What should you remember?

- We are twice as motivated to avoid loss than we are to gain something.
- We call this the Loss Aversion principle.

What can you do?

- Frame the desired behavior as preventing loss.
- Ask yourself what people will lose if they do not do the desired behavior and communicate this loss in your online message.

We value something more if a noticeable effort has been put into it

HOW TO BOOST MOTIVATION
Perceived value

If you are looking for the cheapest flight, there are plenty of comparison sites that list the ticket prices of all the airlines for you. They usually need some search time to do so. Or rather, they pretend that they do. But you don't mind at all. This makes you feel that they are busy comparing and calculating especially for you.

You've probably been there: when you have finally made your choices and expectantly clicked 'Compare', you have to wait ten seconds. In the meantime, the creators of the site show you the logos of all the companies they are including in their comparison. And that, right there, is the crux of the matter. The reason for the logo parade has everything to do with perceived value: the value that our brain assigns to a product or service. This is an emotional value, which partly determines the price that visitors are ultimately willing to pay:

Comparing all airlines

More effort = more value
To put it simply: we assign more value to something when noticeable effort has been put into it. In psychology, we call this the Perceived Value principle.

The fact that the comparison site needs some time gives us the feeling that it is doing its utmost to find the most affordable ticket. As a result, our confidence in the site grows and we are less inclined to order our ticket somewhere else.

This obviously doesn't mean that you should immediately start building delays into your environment as well. Below, we have listed two natural ways you can use the Perceived-Value Principle to further motivate your visitors.

Show that you're making an effort...

The first way is for you to show that you're making an effort. IKEA does this cleverly: they increase the perceived value among visitors with videos in which IKEA employees show how much effort they put into making self-assembly easy for the customer. We see them designing the products in great detail, trying, adjusting and trying again, so that visitors almost automatically assign more value to the products.

If you want to apply the Perceived Value principle in your online environment, try creating a making-of video, for example. Or use numbers to express how many people, machines and time your products or services require to be produced. There is a good chance that the perceived value will increase, and with it the chance that your visitors will want to pay the price that you ask.

... and let your visitors make an effort

Another way is to get your visitors to put some effort into something. Here again, we are looking at IKEA. For many people, assembling a small cupboard is quite a task. However, once you have it on display in a room, it's more satisfying than if you had had it delivered ready-made. So, we attach more value to the cupboard. We call this the 'IKEA effect'.

You can achieve the same result online. You could get your visitors to play (and win) a simple game before rewarding them with a discount. Or have them assemble your product online, just like you can with Nike shoes. If you do this, your visitors will be extra motivated to take the next step towards conversion.

 The advice
Show how much effort you're putting in, And get your visitors to put some effort in

MOTIVATION VERSUS ABILITY

Do the ticket comparison sites in the example really need that much time to retrieve, process and present that data? Or do you think they *deliberately* slow down this process? In the latter case, there is a field of tension between, on the one hand, increasing motivation through more perceived value, and, on the other hand, lowering the ability because it takes longer. With an experiment such as an A/B test, you can find out what weighs more heavily in your case and yields the best conversion.

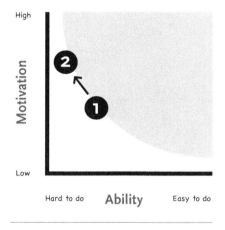

Motivation-enhancing content can reduce ability, thus undoing the positive effect on conversion, or even lowering it.

What should you remember?

- We value something more if a noticeable effort has been put into it.
- This applies to the effort that we put in ourselves, and the effort that others have put in.
- We call this the 'Perceived Value principle'.

What can you do?

- Show how much effort you are putting in
- and let your visitors put effort into something.

We are more likely to adapt our behavior if we are given a reason to do so

HOW TO BOOST MOTIVATION

Reasons why

You are getting ready for an appointment but need to quickly copy some documents. However, there's a big line of people waiting for the copier. What do you do? You ask if you can skip the line. There is a good chance that this approach will work. As long as you give a reason, that is.

In her famous 'copy machine study', Harvard professor Ellen Langer investigated whether providing a reason will get you priority at a copy machine.[27] And if so: what reasons? She asked the people in the line three different questions.

The first group of waiting people were asked a question without reason:

- Excuse me, I have five pages. May I use the Xerox machine?

The second group got the same question, but with a good reason:

- Excuse me, I have five pages. May I use the Xerox machine, because I'm in a rush?

The third group got the same question again, but with a completely idiotic reason:

- Excuse me, I have five pages. May I use the Xerox machine, because I have to make copies?

The result? Of the waiting people who were asked the question without a reason, 60 percent let the person go first. If the question came with a good reason, 94 percent stepped aside. And now for the good part: when asked with a completely idiotic reason, 93 percent of those waiting still let the person go first. Langer concluded that it doesn't matter what reason you give, as long as you give a reason. The word 'because' appeals to our need to have a reason for something and is, therefore, sufficient to motivate people. We call this the 'Reasons Why principle'.

AS OR BECAUSE?

There is hardly any difference in meaning between the conjunctions 'as' and 'because'. Still, 'because' is the best choice if you want to convince people. Our brain registers a message after 'because' as a fact, and a message after 'as' usually as an opinion. And facts usually affect our behavior more strongly than opinions.

Coming up with reasons

So, if you want to increase the motivation of your visitors, consider what reasons they may have to display the behavior you want. Why do they download an app? Why do they buy a product? Why do they sign up for a newsletter? Try to focus on good reasons, because with good reasons you not only motivate people, you will actually help them too. Next, list the most likely motives and give them a prominent place in your design.

In practice

We successfully applied the Reasons Why principle for a large comparison website of energy companies. To motivate visitors to use this website in their search for an energy company, we came up with the following three reasons:

- Choose this website, because you will save up to $300.
- Choose this website, because throwing money away is such a waste.
- Choose this website, because in two minutes you'll know how much you're saving.

Highlighting these three reasons together had the desired effect: a conversion increase of 5 percent. Reason enough to try this principle for yourself, right?

 Consider what (good) reasons your visitors have to do the behavior you want and make these reasons part of your design

What should you remember?

- We are more likely to adapt our behavior if we are given a reason to do so.
- In principle, it does not matter what the reason is, but above all that a reason is mentioned.
- With a good reason, you will obviously help your visitors better than with a bad reason.
- We call this the 'Reasons Why principle'.

What can you do?

- Consider what (good) reasons your visitors have to do the behavior you want and make these reasons part of your design.

Part 4

How to increase ability

HOW TO INCREASE ABILITY

What is ability?

In addition to prompts and motivation, the Fogg Behavior Model contains a third factor that determines our behavior: ability. In short, it is about the extent to which someone is *capable* of doing something. By making the desired behavior easier to do, you increase people's ability. And, therefore, the chances of conversion.

You may recognize this: sometimes you are pretty motivated to do something, but in the end you don't do it. According to BJ Fogg there is only a single cause: the behavior is too difficult, the ability is too low. Say you're excited about a pair of shoes you've seen online, for example. As soon as you want to check out, however, you are asked to first create an account. And come up with a secure password of at least nine characters. Including a capital letter, a number and... Oh, never mind. The shoes weren't that amazing anyway.

When something is too difficult, we tend to give up on it or postpone it. We only persevere if we are sufficiently motivated. And vice versa: if something is very easy, we tend to do it. Even if we're barely motivated.

Crucial insight for behavior designers

This is a crucial insight for behavior designers. It doesn't matter whether or not your target group is highly motivated: by making desirable behavior more feasible, you will, by definition, increase the chances that your visitors will implement it. And, therefore, the chances of conversion.

In the following chapters, we will show you the practical principles you can use to achieve this. However, in order to understand what these principles are based on, it is useful to find out, first of all, which factors determine whether something is difficult or not. Here again, we follow the model and philosophy of BJ Fogg. According to him, there are five factors that determine ability:

- physical effort
- mental effort
- time
- routine
- money

These factors can be seen as resources. How easy a behavior is, is determined by the factor of which you have the least. For example, if a behavior takes 10 minutes of time and you don't have time, the behavior is too difficult.
These five factors can be seen as the links in a chain. The weakest link determines what makes a behavior difficult to do.

1. **Reduce the physical effort**
    The first factor that determines our ability is physical effort. In order to do something, we usually have to perform physical actions. They can be big, like going to the gym, but also small, like taking your phone out of your pocket. You will understand that the less physical effort the desired behavior requires from us, the easier it is to display that behavior. This is why you should limit the physical effort your visitors have to make in order to do the desired behavior.

2. **Limit the mental effort**
    In addition to physical effort, there is also mental effort: from understanding and reading to calculating and choosing. The more time it takes to

think about something, the more difficult we find it. As a behavior designer, you have to limit the mental effort. The less your visitors have to think, the greater the chances of achieving the desired behavior.

3 **Ask for as little time as possible**
Time also determines whether we do something or not. Most of us lead very busy lives. It goes without saying that something that takes up much time is more difficult for us. And that reduces the chance that we will exhibit the desired behavior. Take a 25-page survey, for example. You will undoubtedly be able to think of better ways to spend your time. So don't ask your visitors for too much time.

4 **Hold on to habits**
Unknown tasks require more from us than tasks we are used to. That's why we prefer to hold on to our habits rather than exhibit new behavior. It's a lot easier to buy something in a trusted webshop than in a new one. So use the habits of your visitors to facilitate the desired behavior.

5 **Consider the money factor**
It's a well-known expression: money doesn't buy happiness. Still, money makes behavior easier. Purchasing a second car is a lot easier for a person with sufficient financial means than for someone who has less to spend. So, take the money factor into account. Even if you can't lower the price, you can make it seem less 'expensive'.

Simple is not the same for everyone

Specific behavior can be simple for one person and difficult for the next. For example, a 12-year-old child is usually very adept with a PlayStation, because they grew up with it. Grandpa, on the other hand, can barely handle it, because he didn't grow up with it and he doesn't get around to playing as much. The same game of FIFA is, therefore, easier for the grandchild than for grandpa. On the other hand, grandpa will find it much easier to pay for Super Bowl tickets.

When designing an online environment, as a behavior designer you will want to determine what makes the desired behavior difficult for your specific target group. Maybe it is lack of time? In that case, you have to make the behavior more achievable by making sure it takes less time. Are there any financial barriers to the desired behavior? Then you have to concentrate on breaking through them. In other words, increasing ability not only varies from behavior to behavior, but also from visitor to visitor. We noticed that online sellers often choose to make their product or service cheaper, which is by no means always the best choice to make behavior easier. Sometimes your visitors hardly care whether they have to pay $9 or $10 for something (the money factor), as long as the ordering process goes smoothly (the time factor).

Reducing mental effort in particular

When we're online, we hardly need to make any physical effort. Clicking a button burns less than a calorie. In the worst case, we have to whip out our wallet, because we don't know our credit card number off by heart. Or we have to find our passport to make a scan.

This is why, as a behavior designer, you will mainly influence the mental effort of your visitors. Reading and understanding product information, putting together a product, choosing from multiple options: it requires a lot of thinking. And that is what you can often minimize. That is why we pay particular attention to this in this book.

In the next few chapters, we discuss twelve practical ways to make behavior easier:

- **Reduce options**
  Reduce the number of options you show at the same time.

- **Offer decision aid**
  Help your visitors choose, for example, by categorizing, differentiating, filtering or using a wizard

- **Default, prefill and autocomplete**
  Select a default option for each choice in the customer journey, enter information in advance, and speed up data entry by making suggestions.

- **The Jenga technique**
  See which headings, phrases and paragraphs you can leave out.

- **Remove distractions**
  Eliminate everything that distracts from the desired behavior.

- **Provide feedback**
  Eliminate doubt at all points in the customer journey with quick, proper feedback.

- **Offer reversibility**
  Emphasize the reversibility of the choices that your visitors can make.

- **Page structure**
  Organize your information using hierarchy and rhythm within a single column, and place together what belongs together.

- **Don't make me think**
  Save your visitors thinking and research work.

- **Familiarity**
  Use design patterns that visitors are familiar with.

- **Anticipated effort**
  Reduce the expected effort by making it clear that a task will not take much effort or time at all.

- **Making undesirable behavior more difficult**
  Make behavior that is undesirable for you or your visitors extra difficult.

All the examples we give with these principles have little to do with unconscious influence, which is what the part about motivation was all about. Ability is primarily about practical measures. By applying these correctly in your online environment, you are guaranteed to make the desired behavior easier, and you can increase your conversion.

Choosing from many options requires a lot of mental effort and can lead to us not choosing

HOW TO INCREASE ABILITY

Reduce options

When you ask people whether they like having lots of options, they usually answer yes. However, hard sales figures show that offering lots of options is often bad for conversion. So, we sometimes choose not to choose at all.

Take the menu in a restaurant, for example. Some menus feature dozens of entrees. There is something to take every guest's fancy and nobody gets bored of the offer. However, just try choosing from all these delicious options.

Granted, most people won't leave the restaurant for that reason. Eating out is a special occasion, after all, and choosing an entree is part of the experience. In an online environment, however, you run the risk that your visitors will leave your website or app. If it becomes too difficult and their motivation is not big enough, they give up choosing and postpone their decision.

A well-known study in this field is that of psychologists Sheena Iyengar and Mark Lepper.[28] They tested two situations in a shop that sells jam. In the first, customers were offered 24 different flavors of jam, in the second only six. The difference in sales figures was staggering: customers who could choose from six flavors, bought a whopping ten times more preserves than customers who had the choice of thirty flavors.

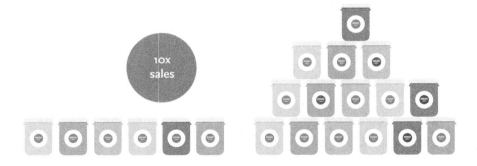

The paradox of choice

This result is also known as the paradox of choice, or, in other words: having many options can lead to a situation where we do not make a choice and postpone the decision. This choice stress appears to become even stronger when the options are similar. A word of caution: we are talking about options that are offered *simultaneously*.

This is valuable information for behavior designers, and something you can easily take into account. Options can almost always be reduced. Compare, for example, the two variants of this page of Unbounce, where you can sign up for a free demo. In the variant where just one registration date less is shown, the conversion rate is almost 17 percent higher.[29]

👍 **Less choice**
More conversion

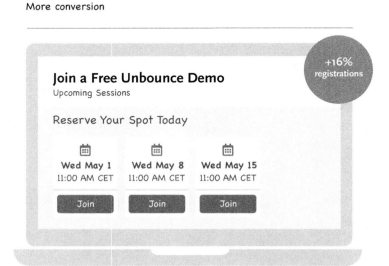

👎 **More choice**
Less conversion

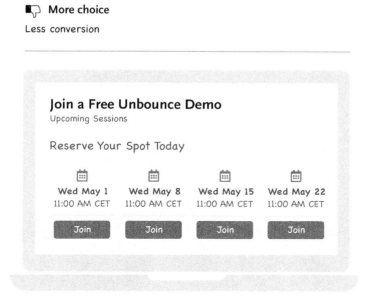

Delete options
Your task as a behavior designer is clear: follow the customer journey of your visitors and look for places where they are asked to choose from more than three options at the same time. If you reduce the number of options in those places, chances are that your conversion will increase. Please note that these should be places where your visitors are likely to find it difficult to choose. If you ask about their country of origin, they will probably know the answer straight away; reducing choice options will have hardly any effect in this case.

Offer options in a different way
Incidentally, you don't always have to delete options. Sometimes, it's fine to choose to offer fewer options at the same time. Suppose you have a web shop that sells shoes. There is a good chance that your visitors will have less trouble choosing in the left-hand variant than the one on the right:

👍 **Show fewer options at the same time**
Makes chosing easier

👎 **Showing many options at the same time**
Can lead to choice stress

In the left-hand variant, you start by showing the three categories. Next, you show only the five best-selling pairs per category and 'hide' the rest behind a click. Just as many options, but a lot easier to choose.

In short: be aware that making a choice is difficult and that it requires mental effort from your visitors. Reduce the number of options that you offer at the same time to save your visitors choice stress and increase their ability.

 Reduce the number of options that you show at the same time

What should you remember?

- Choosing from many options requires a lot of brainpower.
- This can lead to not choosing at all.
- This is especially true when the options are similar.

What can you do?

- Reduce the number of options you show at the same time.
- Preferable offer three, but no more than five, options for each step in the customer journey.
- One way to do this is to delete options.
- Another way is to categorize your choices, for example by first showing the three or five most important choices, and hiding the rest behind an additional click.

We choose more easily and quickly when we get some help

HOW TO INCREASE ABILITY
Offer decision aid

Let's go back to that chock-a-block menu from the previous chapter. Seeing as leaving the restaurant is not really an option, you start looking for ways to make a choice anyway. For example, by asking the waiter for help. If the waiter then asks you if you are in the mood for something spicy, sweet, or crunchy, and you know what you want, choosing suddenly becomes much easier.

Choosing is not only difficult because there are often several attractive options, but above all because we always want to make the right choice. Especially when the choice is large or diverse, we often like some assistance, and that's where you come in as a behavior designer. You can help your visitors in the following ways:

- categorize;
- filter;
- differentiate;
- invest in the magic of wizards.

We'll take you through them one by one.

Categorize
A first way to help your visitors choose is to categorize, by grouping all the options that belong together for one reason or another. For example, you can group a range of online courses into:

- courses for beginners;
- courses for advanced learners;
- courses for experts.

If your shop sells phones, you can categorize devices into:

- iPhone devices;
- Android devices;
- Pixel devices.

From shape, color and type to price, popularity and lifespan: there are many ways to categorize options. Involve people from your target group to figure out what the most important selection criterion is.

Differentiate

A second way to help people make a choice is to differentiate. Choice stress is often caused by options that are too similar. If we can't see the difference, we get stuck and postpone our choice.

One way to differentiate is to create price differences. For example, if you have to pay exactly the same amount for two comparable packs of chewing gum, choosing is difficult. But if you increase the price of one of them by a few cents, the price factor suddenly becomes an argument. This makes the choice easier:

👍 **Price difference**
Makes choosing easier: 77% buys chewing gum.

👎 **Exactly the same price**
Makes choosing harder: 46% buys chewing gum.

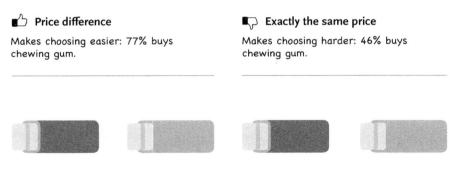

If you offer products that are very similar, highlight the differences in your design. Don't focus on the USPs they have in common, but name the differences.

Filter

Filtering is a third way to make choosing easier: offer your visitors the option to check or uncheck options or features. This allows people to limit their choices themselves. As an online behavior designer, you can do this by designing a classic filter menu with tags.

We applied such a filter ourselves for a large web shop for white goods. We opted for a quick filter, because our experience shows that complex filters overshoot the mark and, therefore, do not make the choice any easier.

To find out what people base their choice on for a new washing machine, we asked a random group of one hundred people which three things they consider most important when purchasing a washing machine. From this survey we distilled a list of ten properties, such as 'large drum', 'super silent' and 'fast spin'. Next, we designed a quick filter. With a single click, visitors were given an overview of, for example, all low-noise washing machines. Below, you can see the quick filter in the left column.

It was a minor adjustment with major consequences: after introducing this quick filter, the number of people who made a choice increased by 25 percent.

Wizards

Working with wizards is an attractive way to filter choices. Wizards are tools that allow visitors to put together their own product. After filling in their individual wishes, the tool conjures up the end result. In this way, you do not reduce your visitors' choice step by step, but instead present the result of the choices they have made in one go.

You can creatively 'package' such a wizard in the form of a short interview: you ask your visitors to answer a few questions, for example about how they use their phone. Based on these wishes, various models are automatically out. This makes the choice easier.

More conversion and improved customer experience

We already wrote this at the start of the chapter: choosing is difficult. Our brain is not wired to choose from many options at the same time. That's why we generally like a little help. Choice assistance not only leads to better conversion, but also to an improved customer experience.

 Help your visitors choose by, for example, categorizing, differentiating, filtering or using a wizard

What should you remember?

- We choose more easily and quickly when we get some assistance
- Decision aids are a way to reduce the mental effort of choosing.

What can you do?

- Help your visitors choose, for example, by categorizing, differentiating, or filtering.
- One attractive form of filtering is using a wizard.

If we don't have a clear preference, we often choose the default option

HOW TO INCREASE ABILITY

Default, prefill and autocomplete

When it became apparent in 2009 that students in The Netherlands were increasingly struggling with sky-high student loans, the Dutch government wanted to halt this trend. Not with a very costly campaign, but by making subtle adjustments. Changing the default option on the application form proved sufficient.

On the DUO (Dutch Education Executive) website, where students can apply for a student loan, the students were initially offered the maximum loan amount. Rather than just 'an' option, this was the standard option. Borrowing less was also an option, for which the students needed to actively tick a lower loan amount.

The government decided to change that. From now on, after their performance-related education grant, students were no longer offered the maximum loan amount as standard, but the much lower amount they had received in the last month of their performance-related education grant. To borrow more, they had to actively adjust the loan amount. This small adjustment had a huge impact: the percentage of students who opted for the maximum loan amount fell from 68% to 11% in two years.[30]

In online environments we call pre-set standard options like this the 'default'. If visitors do not have a clear preference or are not entirely sure about a choice, they often choose the default option. They assume that experts have determined that option with the best intentions and that it is, therefore, also the best choice.

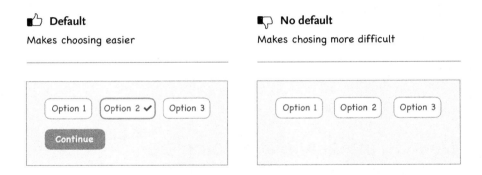

Two sides of the default

As an online behavior designer, you can use this to your advantage. If you do so in a customer-friendly way, you select a standard option that is (probably) the best for your visitors. Changing the default option on the DUO website is a good example of this.

However, you can also guide your visitors in the direction that is best for you. Take a comparison site, for example, that puts the result that will earn the website itself the most at the top of the results list. Customer friendliness is certainly not the starting point in that case.

We ourselves have used the default once or twice to guide visitors in a certain direction. On the website of a lottery we made 'Buy three lottery tickets' the default option, rather than the usual 'Buy one lottery ticket'. This adjustment immediately increased the average order value, but ultimately adversely affected sales because in the long term, fewer people came back to participate in the lottery.

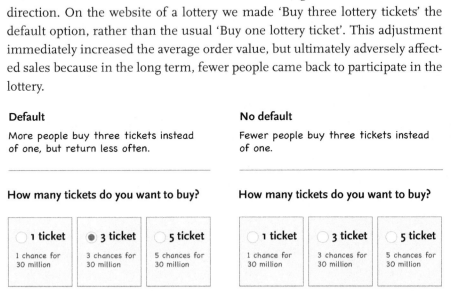

Facilitate the choice process

We see defaults primarily as a means to facilitate visitors' choice process. Ultimately, this is what leads to increased chances of conversion. By adding default options to your design, you minimize the risk of doubt and reduce choice stress.

Always choose a default option that closely matches the needs of your visitors. By doing so, you save them actions and thinking, and they never make a really 'wrong' choice. So, you should design your online decision environment in such a way that the standard outcome makes your visitors happy.

Variant: prefill

One form of default is prefill: filling in the most probable choice in advance, often based on stored data. By prefilling the home address as a delivery address in an online form, or pre-selecting your visitor's most likely country as the country of origin, you save your visitors time and effort:

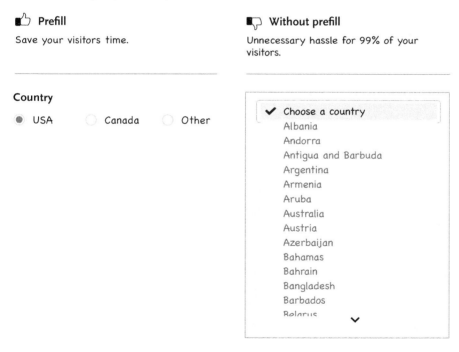

Uber is an example of a company that makes ordering behavior easier. If you often book the same type of taxi, after a while the app will make that ride the default. In this way, Uber makes it easier for you to display the desired behavior: booking a taxi ride:

Variant: autocomplete

Another form of default is autocomplete: complete entered data automatically. For example, if you enter a search query on Google, the search engine often knows what you mean after only three characters. Not because the creators know you personally, but because a million others have asked the same question before.

By showing visitors the most common search terms after entering a part of the search term, Google saves visitors thinking time. There is a good chance that 'their' search term is in amongst the others, so that all they have to do is click on it. There's an additional effect: the fact that you are apparently not the only person with that search query is a form of social proof. And that also makes you more motivated. (See chapter *Social Proof* in part 3.)

Default: always a good idea

If, after reading this chapter, you would like to start working with default, pre-fill and autocomplete, start by finding the moments in your customer journey when your visitors have to make a choice between two or more options. Then decide whether you can make one of those options the default. It's a good idea to do this wherever possible. When you use a default, visitors are more likely to choose the desired option; and to make a choice at all. So, setting the default will positively affect your conversion by definition.

 Set a default for each choice in the customer journey, prefill information and speed up entering data by autocompleting suggestions

'PEOPLE LIKE YOU'

The more you know about your visitors, the better you understand them and the better you can help them. If you have a large number of visitors, use the data to prefill information based on 'people like you'.

What should you remember?

- If we don't have a clear preference, we often choose the default option.
- In an online decision-making environment, we call the standard option the 'default'.
- With a default, you can save your visitors mental effort.
- It also prevents them from making the 'wrong' choice.
- Prefill means entering the desired option in advance, often based on stored data.
- Autocomplete means automatic completion of entered data.

What can you do?

- Select a default option for each choice in the customer journey.
- Prefill information.
- Speed up entering data by autocompleting suggestions.

We find it easier to read a text if it does not contain unnecessary words

HOW TO INCREASE ABILITY
The Jenga technique

You've probably played Jenga before. The idea is to take out as many wooden blocks as possible from a tower without it falling over. So, to win, you have to know where to 'demolish'. You can use that principle as an online behavior designer when writing your texts.

As you now know, increased ability ensures that visitors display the desired behavior faster. That's why, as an online behavior designer, it's a good idea to eliminate any distracting factors. Deleting superfluous text is a good example. We find it easier to read a text if it does not contain unnecessary words. The best way to do this is by using a technique we developed ourselves: the Jenga technique.

Valuable seconds
Before we explain exactly how this technique works, we will briefly dive into some numbers. Did you know that sometimes it takes our brains 250 milliseconds to process a word? Quite literally: a fraction of a second. That may sound pretty fast, but usually a word is just a part of a sentence, a paragraph and a page.

Take a web page of 250 words, for example: reading it takes more than a minute. In a book or magazine a minute may not be much, but online it is an eternity. A lot can happen during that time to interrupt your visitor's customer journey, like an incoming phone call, a child that starts to cry or a parcel delivery person at the door. To reduce the risk of distraction, it is, therefore, important to keep your copy short and to the point.

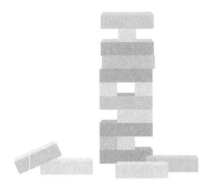

Demolishing words

So, where does Jenga come into this? Think of the message you want to convey as a tower. The message is often written with an unnecessary amount of words. Just like with Jenga, you can 'demolish' many of them. Let's analyze the following sentence:

- Do you want more conversion on your website?

Do you need all the words in that sentence to understand the message? To ask the question is to answer it. Here's another way:

- Want more conversion?

From eight to three words: much shorter, and also clearer and more powerful. For the Jenga technique, we use the rule of thumb that you can shorten the initial version of a text by half.

From 76 to 27 words

The previous example is about short copy, but the Jenga technique also works for longer texts. Take a look at how we reduce the text below from 72 to 23 words:

- When you write a sentence, or maybe even an entire text, a lot of words come to mind and before you know it you often create something that is just a bit too long. That's why we advise you to find words that you can simply omit. In most cases you will find that you can often easily leave out more than 50 percent of the words. They are completely redundant.

- **When you write** ~~a sentence, or maybe even an entire text, a lot of words come to mind and before you know it~~ **you often create something** ~~that is just a bit~~ **too long.** ~~That's why we advise you to~~ **find the words that you can** ~~just~~ **leave out.** ~~In most cases you will find that~~ ~~you can~~ **often** ~~easily leave out~~ **more than 50 percent** ~~of the words. They are completely redundant.~~

- When you write, you often create something too long. Find the words that you can leave out. Often more than 50 percent.

Removing redundancy

Good Jenga players manage to take out superfluous blocks without the tower falling over. The same goes for good online behavior designers: they can take away unnecessary words without making the text unclear.

Incidentally, that doesn't mean you should leave out 'as many' words as possible. Just like with Jenga, it is about removing what we call 'redundancy' in psychology: abundance. Therefore, always put yourself in your visitors' shoes and check for each text whether a word or sentence adds something that's important enough.

> **TIP: ORGANIZE A JENGA SESSION**
> Sometimes it is quite difficult to delete texts in which you have put your heart and soul. That is why it can be useful to involve 'blank' team members. Organize a joint Jenga session and let others demolish your text, as it were.

Finally, a word of caution. On product pages, visitors usually do want to read a lot about a product. On those pages, your proverbial tower is more likely to fall over if you remove information. On this type of page it is okay to explain a lot, but keep it compact. The same applies to long reads in content marketing.

 See which headings, phrases and paragraphs you can leave out

What should you remember?

- We find it easier to read a text if it does not contain unnecessary words.
- We call deleting unnecessary words and sentences the Jenga technique.
- It makes your text shorter and, therefore, more readable.

What can you do?

- See which headings, phrases and paragraphs you can leave out.
- Our rule of thumb: you can usually shorten the initial version of a text by 50 percent.
- Do not delete too enthusiastically in product pages.

We find it hard to concentrate when we are distracted by elements that have nothing to do with our task

HOW TO INCREASE ABILITY
Remove distractions

You are busy making a calculation, but your colleagues keep asking you questions. Or you are reading a white paper, but your partner's music is too loud. Or you are writing a book, but the phone keeps ringing. All these distractions have an inhibiting effect on your behavior. Offline, but certainly also online.

The previous chapter explains how the Jenga technique helps you to delete superfluous text. However, eliminating unnecessary content goes further than just text. Your visitors are slowed down by all the distracting elements that have nothing to do with the desired behavior.

Surely it can't hurt? Think again!
Many online designers add all kinds of content to their landing and product pages, like the company news, the three most-read blogs, or the latest posts on social media. In other words: content that doesn't really matter on that page. Consciously or unconsciously, these designers may think: surely it can't hurt?

But is this true? Earlier in this book, we said that competing prompts cause unnecessary distraction. This is how you should see all that extra content: as elements that demand additional brain power from your visitors. Not only when they consume that content, but also if they ignore it; which also requires mental effort. In other words: surely it will hurt.

In practice
A conversion manager at a major bank recently shared his success story with us. By way of experiment, he had removed the introductions on a large number of web pages. Most of them were superfluous; they were only there because there was a mandatory input field in the content management system (the

'backend' of the website). It turned out to be a golden move: overall lead conversion increased by more than 10 percent.

Another example is the SimCity website. Removing the promotional banner resulted in 43 percent more sales:

👍 **Without banner**
Removing unnecessary distractions resulted in 43% more checkouts.

👎 **With banner**
Unnecessary distraction can harm conversation.

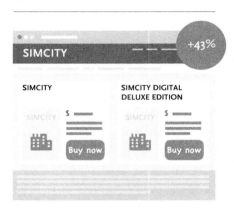

Focus on the desired behavior
To increase your visitors' ability, and consequently the chances of conversion, it is best to focus on the desired behavior. One way to do this is by offering only one option. Everything else – from images and navigation menus to downloads and clicks – only distracts visitors. So, for example, if your visitors enter a payment screen, don't distract them with alternative products, but let them settle their bill in peace.

Kill your darlings
We can almost hear you thinking: what about my precious online environment, will there be anything left of it? Unfortunately, sometimes content must indeed bite the dust, to remove distractions. And sometimes it hurts. Nevertheless, be strict with yourself, and kill your darlings. Determine what most visitors come for and pave the way for them. Try to see the removal of distracting content as a party. It is the cheapest way to increase your conversion.

TRIMMING

When removing distracting content, it sometimes helps to assume a different identity and examine your own work from a distance. You could also ask other people to put themselves in your visitors' shoes and help you to 'trim' your online environment.

 Eliminate everything that distracts from the desired behavior.

What should you remember?

- We find it hard to concentrate when we are distracted by elements that have nothing to do with our task.

What can you do?
- Eliminate everything that distracts from the desired behavior.
- Focus your design on the desired behavior and the path towards it.

We need confirmation to know
if we're on the right track

HOW TO INCREASE ABILITY
Provide feedback

Imagine throwing an apple over your shoulder. You wait a few seconds and you hear a dull thump. But what if you don't hear anything? Exactly: that's when doubt strikes. Did that apple actually land?

When we press a key on our keyboard, we expect a letter to appear on the screen. If we press a light switch, a light should come on. And when we throw an apple over our shoulder, there should be a sound that confirms the landing of the apple. If we don't get that feedback, we can't explain what's going on and we get confused.

In short: we need confirmation when we perform behavior.

Feedback motivates ...
Earlier in this book, we explained how to use feedback to motivate visitors to do the desired behavior. (See the *Confetti Shower* chapter in part 3.) From green check marks to compliments: every pat on the back stirs up and sustains positive emotions. As a result, your visitors will experience every step of their customer journey as a party. This will motivate them to keep going.

... and increase the ability
But feedback has another function within behavior design: you can also use feedback to make navigating your online environment feel more natural and, therefore, easier. On the one hand, by continuously providing feedback on what visitors have done, on the other hand by letting them know whether what they did was right or wrong. With this feedback, you increase your visitors' ability, and, therefore, your chances of conversion.

Confirmation throughout the customer journey

While online, your customers are constantly throwing apples over their shoulders; and every time they want to hear that the apple has landed. It's up to you to give them that confirmation. This allows them to continue their customer journey without any doubts. Here are some examples of various moments during the customer journey:

- The message 'This password is strong enough' when they come up with a decent password.
- The friendly error message if a form field is filled in incorrectly or not completely.
- The pop-up window indicating that an action has been successful.
- The progress indicator that shows which steps have been completed and which are still to come.
- The email confirmation after an online order.

Eliminate uncertainty

The general rule applies: the more uncertain a visitor is, the more feedback you should give. Don't worry about exaggerating. Especially when it comes to crucial choices in the customer journey, visitors like to know things for sure.

They are most in need of feedback when they have to decide whether to buy a product. Did I select the right size? Did I remove that one blouse from my shopping cart or not? And did I enter the correct address? By giving people the opportunity to check all the above, you almost always eliminate the uncertainty.

Take booking a plane ticket, for example. Most travelers know that you need to enter your passport details error-free to prevent problems and ridiculously high costs for changes. Online behavior designers at an airline should, therefore, continue to show the passport details during the booking process. Or, at the very least, give their visitors the opportunity to constantly check the entered data.

Negative feedback

Visitors are just people. And people make mistakes, for example when filling in a form field. At these times, you need to give negative feedback: not judgmental or bossy, but helpful and motivating. Or, if you want to get it completely right: by complimenting.

Judgmental
Email address missing!

Bossy
Enter a valid email address.

Helpful and motivating
We need your email address to send you a confirmation. For example: john@example.nl.

Complimenting
You have completed everything perfectly, now we just need your email address. We need it to send you a confirmation email. For example: john@example.nl.

The first example is distinctly negative feedback. You wouldn't shout 'No sugar!' at your server when there's no sugar in your coffee. The second example has room for improvement as well. 'Valid', for example, is a typical IT word. And let's be honest: how do you feel about people who constantly bark commands at you? The third example clearly shows that you want to help your visitors. Moreover, you immediately make it clear what they still need to do. It's friendly, right? But the fourth example is the most sociable. It focuses on everything that has gone well so far. With a little goodwill, you can also 'frame' an error message as a compliment.

At all times

Whether it's positive or negative feedback: as a behavior designer, you need to make sure that your visitors never have to wonder whether they are performing well. Every moment they have to spend thinking about that, comes at the expense of the time you have to entice them into the desired behavior.

Analyze your customer journey and design feedback for all actions or input from your visitor. It is a good idea to make your feedback visible immediately after an action and continue to show it as the customer journey progresses. The following applies to each step: the faster the confirmation, the more confidently your visitor will continue the customer journey.

 Eliminate doubt at every stage of the customer journey with quick, good feedback

What should you remember?

- We need confirmation to know if we're on the right track.
- One form of confirmation is feedback.
- Feedback after an action means that your visitors do not have to think about whether they are doing things right.

What can you do?

- Eliminate doubt at all points in the customer journey with quick, proper feedback.
- The more uncertain your visitors are, the more feedback you have to give them.
- Give your visitors negative feedback as well, but do so in a helpful and motivating way, or even with compliments.

We're less insecure if we know
we can undo our behavior

HOW TO INCREASE ABILITY

Offer reversibility

Chances are that several newsletters clutter your inbox every day, or your spam folder, as the case may be. This is partly because we subscribe to newsletters without any difficulty. But why do we do this? As it happens, we do it mainly because this behavior is reversible.

Reversibility is all about the certainty that we can reverse a purchase if we regret it afterwards. If we know we can go back, we are a lot less afraid of doing something. This increases the chances of conversion.

Cancellation, unsubscribe options, exchange guarantees: in the online world, more and more companies are discovering the power of reversibility. They will tell you, for example:

- You can unsubscribe with one click.
- Free, easy returns within 14 days.
- You can cancel your subscription free of charge at any time.
- You can cancel the hotel reservation free of charge up to 24 hours in advance.
- Money back guarantee, no questions asked.

Don't be afraid
Product managers are sometimes reluctant to communicate reversibility. They think: let's not put ideas in the visitors' heads about returning their orders. This is understandable, because returns are a costly business. We wrote earlier, however, that behavior design is not the same as designing a message. By highlighting reversibility, you increase the conversion. And what's more: if you don't communicate this reversibility clearly, your competitor will.

Large web shops like The Gap and Amazon know this too. That is why their customers can return their products free of charge and super easy. In fact, reversibility has become a prominent part of their persuasion strategy. But by helping and informing visitors extremely well in making choices, for example for the right size, a lot less products are returned. This will benefit everyone.

At the transaction and interface level

So far, we have been talking about applications of transaction-level reversibility. But as an online behavior designer, you can also use this principle to optimize your online environment at the interface level. You can do this, for example, by giving your visitors the opportunity to adjust their order at every step of the customer journey. Or by making sure that they can always go back a step without having to re-enter their data.

Being able to take a step back comes in handy for visitors who make a mistake. The 'Undo' function (control-z) was one of the main reasons to replace typewriters by PCs with printers.

How to apply reversibility

To apply reversibility, start by analyzing your customer journey. Find out where you invite visitors to do behavior that has a social or financial impact, such as 'Upload your profile picture' or 'Confirm your order'. Come up with texts that emphasize the reversibility of that choice.

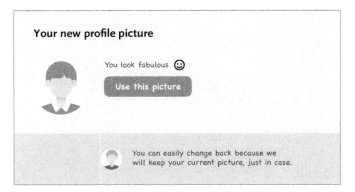

 Emphasize the reversibility of the choices that your visitors can make

What should you remember?

- We're less uncertain if we know we can undo our behavior.
- You can apply reversibility at the transaction level and at the interface level.

What can you do?

- Emphasize the reversibility of the choices that your visitors can make.

We like to scan and read
on autopilot

HOW TO INCREASE ABILITY

Page structure

Unclear structures, lost information, hidden calls-to-action: poorly constructed online environments demand a lot from visitors. If it's all just a little too much trouble, they up and leave, probably never to return. This is why a logical page structure of your online environment is essential to entice your visitors towards displaying the desired behavior.

Our brain likes structure. The more logically information is presented to us, the better we can process it. And the easier the behavior is, the greater the chance that it will happen. In this chapter, we will discuss four guidelines that will make it a lot easier for your visitors to scan and understand online pages:

- hierarchy
- rhythm
- columns
- juxtaposition

Hierarchy: as flat as possible
A page should be entirely clear about what is the most important. That's why you should work with 'chapters' and 'sub-chapters' that are clearly distinguishable. Don't design more than those two levels, otherwise things get too complicated. In other words: make the hierarchy as flat as possible:

Do
A flat hierarchy with two levels maximum.

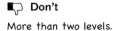 **Don't**
More than two levels.

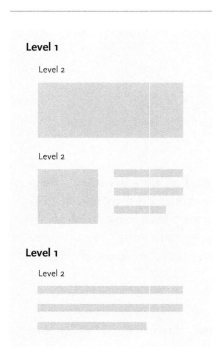

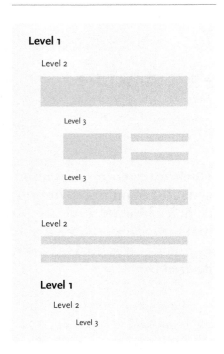

Rhythm: clear and consistent

Rhythm has to do with the visual design of your hierarchy. By organizing blocks of content consistently and rhythmically, your visitors will understand more quickly how the online environment works. As a result, they will navigate it effortlessly.

For example, give each block the same type of top layout, such as the same heading with the same font size in the same place. If your visitors immediately see where one block ends and where the next block begins, they only need to read the headings to determine whether they scroll further or zoom in on the content of a block.

The content varies, but the clear edges of your blocks help your visitors discover the rhythm. To maintain a nice visual rhythm, always keep the distance between the bottom of one block and the top of the next block the same:

👍 Do: rythm

The headings in this example are all the same size and left aligned. The font size of the paragraphs is also consistent. The background colour systematically changes for each block. While scrolling, our brain can decide more easily and quickly where a new block begins. This saves mental effort and increases ability.

👎 Don't: no rythm

The headings in this example have different font sizes and are all differently aligned. The paragraphs also have varying font sizes. While scrolling, our brain has to put in more effort to decide where a new block begins.

Columns: one is preferable to two or three

How to display text forms a dilemma for many online designers. You have probably been there yourself: do you use one, two or maybe three columns? Our advice: if in doubt, always choose one column, unless you have good reasons not to.

Websites with multiple columns are a lot more complicated. There is a reason why mobile interfaces are praised for their simplicity; this is partly due to the fact that it is impossible to use multiple columns. If you use one column, you can control how your visitors navigate through your online environment: from top to bottom and vice versa. If you give your visitors two or more columns, you lose that initiative.

All text in one column: it may not always look great but it requires only minimal mental effort from your visitors. Their eyes can only go one way. With one column, they don't need to decide what to look at. What's more, thanks to their mobile phones, they are already used to scrolling through long one-column pages. This is why a single column is the best choice to increase your visitors' ability:

👍 **Do**
Single column

👎 **Don't**
Multiple columns

Juxtaposition: put together what belongs together

Finally, a word about juxtaposition. 'Juxta' means 'beside' in Latin. Juxtaposition has everything to do with the proximity of elements. The closer they are to each other, the faster we perceive them as a group. And the further apart they are, the sooner we perceive them as separate elements. The image below shows what we mean:

By 'juxtaposing' elements in the right way, your visitors will be able to scan and understand your online page more easily, which means, for example, the following:

- call to action is best placed below or to the right of the persuasive text.
- It is best not to place the heading for a paragraph too far above that paragraph.
- The distance between that heading and the associated content is best made smaller than the distance between the heading and the end of the previous block.

 Do
Make sure the heading is closer to the content to which it applies.

Don't
Headings that are as far away from the content that they belong with as from the content that they don't belong with.

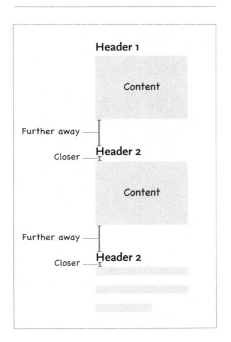

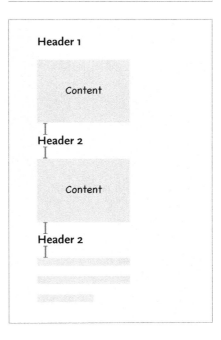

If you fail to do this, it will take the brain a few additional steps to figure out what belongs with what.

This may seem logical, but sometimes designers can't resist going for the originality award. As a result, visitors have to think unnecessarily long.

'USER IN YER FACE'

Belgian design agency Bagaar has a fun take on everything that can go wrong when building a page. On the 'User in yer face' website (userinyerface.com), they have deliberately made every single mistake in online designer repertoire. Take a look at the following example. The check boxes appear to belong to the pictures above them. It's only when you click on them that you realise that they belong with the pictures below them.

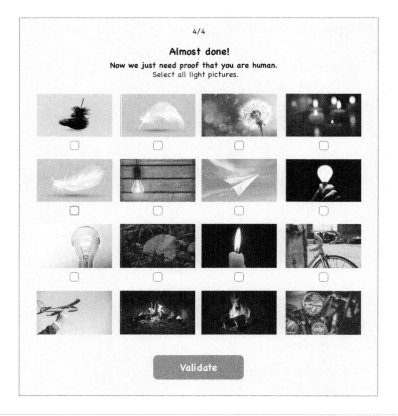

Getting started

If you want to improve the page structure of your existing website, app or mailing, you should make sure that you have mastered the principles of hierarchy, rhythm, columns and juxtaposition. If you are going to design a new online environment, keep these principles in mind right from the start.

 Organize your information using hierarchy and rhythm within one column, and place together what belongs together

What should you remember?

- We like to scan and read on autopilot.
- The more logically information is presented to us, the easier our brains can process it.

What can you do?

- Organize your information using hierarchy and rhythm within a single column, and place together what belongs together.

We like it when we don't have to rack our brains

HOW TO INCREASE ABILITY
Don't make me think

Product pages often state that an order will be delivered 'within three working days'. This is good to know, but you have to calculate it for yourself. Today's Friday, so three days from now makes Tuesday. Or is it Monday? And does today count? Such a hassle.

You'll find out eventually when your order will be delivered, probably fairly quickly too. Still, it takes some thinking or figuring out. The web shop could have saved you the effort if they had told you next Monday or Tuesday.

It may take some effort to program a formula that calculates the expected delivery date based on the time of ordering. But it really pays off. The more thinking steps you perform for your visitors, the greater the ability. And, therefore, the higher your chances of conversion.

Ready-made answers
A smart way to make your visitors think as little as possible is to have information ready. Every thinking and research step you save them, brings them one step closer to clicking, taking action, or purchasing.

We call this principle 'Don't make me think'. It is based on the notion that we like not having to think or think very little for ourselves. American web designer Steve Krug wrote his bestseller with this eponymous title about it in 2005.[31] For you as an online behavior designer, the principle offers countless possibilities to optimize your online environment. In this chapter we discuss three of them:

- Avoid jargon.
- Write from the perspective of your visitors.
- Don't let them do the math.

Avoid jargon

If you want to take out insurance online, chances are that you can choose from 'products'. By this, insurance companies generally refer to the various insurances they offer. Internally, 'products' may be a common term, but externally it raises unnecessary questions. After all, it is unlikely that visitors of your website will think of insurance when they see the word 'product'.

To avoid this kind of ambiguity, it is better to avoid jargon. This is not only professional terminology, but also typical language that employees use among themselves, but that is unclear to the outside world. By speaking your visitors' language, you make it much easier for them to display the desired behavior than when you harass them with meaningless or unknown professional terminology.

- So instead of: *Transaction completed,*
  say *Payment successful.*

- Instead of: *Choose one of the following products,*
  say *Choose your subscription to our newspaper.*

- And instead of: *This field is mandatory,*
  say *Please enter your date of birth.*

Write from the perception of your visitors

As an online behavior designer you do not write for yourself, but for your visitors. Describe explicitly and comprehensibly what something means to them by writing from their perspective. That may sound obvious, but we are naturally inclined to think from our own or our company's perspective, and not from others'. As a result, this often goes wrong in practice.

Take the way in which you present the specifications of a power bank, for example. You can decide to talk about how powerful it is, but then your visitors will still have to figure out for themselves what exactly is in it for them. You can save them the trouble by explicitly indicating how often they can charge their smartphone with it.

- Instead of: *This power bank has a capacity of 20,000 mAh,*

  say: *With this power bank, you can charge your smartphone six to seven times. That's more than an average charger.*

(Most people have no idea whether 20,000 mAh is a lot or a little).

- And instead of: *We have transferred your order number 3434343 to our delivery service,*

say *Your order is on schedule. Your book will be delivered in your letterbox between 14.00 and 16.00 tomorrow.*

(Your visitors are not interested in how your logistics chain works. All they want to know is when to expect what product and whether it fits in the mailbox. That is the perception on which you, as a behavior designer, should focus).

Don't let them do the math

This explicit delivery day is an example of the third way to make your visitors think as little as possible: don't let them do the math. It's better if you do it for them.

- So instead of: *You are 6 miles away from the specified location,*
  say: *From here, it is only 6 minutes by car (6 miles).*

- Instead of: *Order before 11:59 p.m.*
  say: *Order in the next 24 minutes.*

- Instead of: *You still have 4 days, 3 hours and 2 minutes to order*
  say: *Order before July 24th, 21.59 p.m.*

Good to know: if your customer is more than three hours away from a deadline, you should not mention any remaining time. In that case, mentioning the 'order by' time takes less thinking.

Getting started

Applying the 'Don't make me think' principle can be a costly affair. Chances are that you will need to program formulas in order to realize tailor-made calculations. Or to convert product names into spoken language, such as 'your washing machine' instead of 'your Indesit 300 Turbo Plus 45545'. The general rule is: the simpler the interaction at the front-end, the more complicated the development at the back-end. Fortunately, you can start with small adjustments. Run through the customer journey in your online environment. Chances are you'll find opportunities to make your visitors think less.

Save your visitors thinking and research work

What should you remember?

- We like it when we don't have to think too much or too hard.
- Every thinking and research step you save your visitors, brings them one step closer to clicking, taking action, or making a purchase.
- The simpler the front-end, the more complicated the back-end. But your efforts almost always pay off.

What can you do?

- Save your visitors thinking and research work.
- Avoid jargon, write from the perception of your visitors, and don't let them do the math.

We don't need to think as hard when we already know how something works

HOW TO INCREASE ABILITY

Familiarity

The shopping cart? Top right. The clickable company logo that leads to the home page? Top left. And the contact page? Always the last option in the main navigation. Nowadays, many design elements have a fixed position on websites. As an online behavior designer, you want to stick to these conventions.

You could compare it to driving a car: we do this mostly on autopilot; System 1, in other words. If you are an American renting a car in the UK, however, System 1 generally is not going to be enough to get you from A to B. Because all of a sudden, you have to start thinking: drive on the left, change gears on the left, get out on the right hand side. Even though everything is only mirrored, driving immediately becomes a real System-2 activity.

Jakob's Law

Visitors sometimes experience exactly the same thing online. When they visit a website that is not similar to the websites they know, and therefore lacks that recognizable structure, they find it difficult to understand that website. That is why American web-usability pioneer Jakob Nielsen created a tough 'law' for UX designers:

> *"Visitors spend most of their time on other sites, which means they prefer it if your site works the same as all the other sites they already know."*[32]

With Jakob's Law in mind, as an online behavior designer you will want to use design patterns that your visitors are familiar with.

For highly creative people, it can be painful to have to adapt to the masses; with their natural desire for originality, they prefer to design websites according to their own taste, or want to showcase a certain degree of individuality in their design. But to make things easier for their visitors, they too have to conform to Jakob's Law and the Familiarity principle. After all, we are still in the chapter about ability. In other words: the easier the behavior, the greater the chance of conversion.

An infinity of conventions

In the introduction to this chapter, we already highlighted a few conventions that all you online behavior designers had better take into account. In practice, there is an infinite amount of them, all of which more or less emerged of their own accord. Below are a few conventions, for your inspiration:

- Links that are not listed in the main navigation, because they refer to less important items, can be found in the footer.
- In webshops, the product price is displayed above the order button and to the right of the product image.
- In apps, important navigation shortcuts are usually at the bottom.
- Calls to action are listed below the text to which they belong.
- The sub-navigation is usually set up horizontally at the top and otherwise vertically on the left.

We could go on. But you can easily discover the power of familiarity by examining carefully how the most visited and best-known websites have been put together. If you adopt their design patterns, you will most likely be rewarded with a higher conversion.

 Use design patterns that visitors are familiar with

What should you remember?

- We have to make less of a thinking effort if we already know how something works.
- In other words, the more you deviate from the design patterns your visitors are familiar with, the harder you make it for them.
- Conversely, familiar design patterns make it easier for us.
- We call this the 'Familiarity Principle'.

What can you do?

- Use design patterns that visitors are familiar with.
- Analyze the most-visited and best-known websites and adopt their design patterns.

We are more likely to start something if we expect it will take us less effort

HOW TO INCREASE ABILITY

Expected effort

Do you ever get an email with online articles you simply have to read? Even if you don't have a lot of time, you often take a quick look. The intro appeals to you, but you kind of have to leave. And just when you want to click it away, you see 'Reading time: four minutes.' Before you know it, you've started reading anyway.

Stating the reading time of an article is a clever application of the Expected-Effort Principle. If you do this, you facilitate behavior that seems difficult by making it clear that it won't take that much effort or time at all, or less than people might expect. This works especially well with new behavior, when your visitors have to do something they don't know yet.

With text ...
Clever lines of text are a good way to reduce the expected effort. A few examples:

- Reading time: two minutes.
- Creating a profile only takes 30 seconds.
- Your own design in three simple steps.

... and structure
You can also find solutions in the structure with which you offer a task. Suppose your visitors have to register for a program, but that the procedure consists of fifteen steps. If they see this at the beginning, there's a good chance they'll quit straight away. Because fifteen steps: who has the time? But if you divide those fifteen steps into three blocks of five, registering suddenly feels a lot easier. The same goes for long forms: you can often cut them up into smaller pieces as well.

Extra motivation

Chopping up the structure gives you more opportunities to motivate your visitors in additional ways. For example, by treating them to positive feedback at various steps: 'Well done!' (See the chapter *Confetti Shower* in part 3). And by using social proof: '95 percent of our customers configured their bike in two minutes' (See the chapter *Social proof* in part 3.) These are all gentle nudges in the right direction, to start the task.

Also for less motivated visitors

With the Expected Effort principle you can also give less-motivated visitors that last little nudge to proceed to the desired behavior. To do this, clearly indicate from the start that they can pause their task at any time.

If you want to start working with this principle, look for the actions that your visitors dread and that discourage them, such as registration procedures and long forms to complete. By letting them know in those places that the effort is not as bad as it sounds, they will probably get to work sooner. And the beauty of it is that once your visitors have started, there's a good chance that they'll complete their task as well. (See the *Baby Steps* section in Part 2.)

 Reduce the expected effort by making it clear that a task isn't going to take that much effort or time at all

What should you remember?

- We're more likely to start with things that we expect will cost us less effort.
- We call this the 'Expected Effort principle'.
- Once we have started something, there is a good chance we will finish it.

What can you do?

- Reduce the expected effort by making it clear that a task will not take much effort or time at all.
- For example, state the reading time or divide a multitude of steps into smaller blocks, for example with forms.
- Make it clear to less-motivated visitors that they can take a break at any time.

We are more likely to give up
when things get difficult

HOW TO INCREASE ABILITY
Making undesirable behavior more difficult

Have you ever noticed how the order button is often larger and easier to operate than the cancel button? And that the closing button of a pop-up is small compared with the 'Yes, please' button next to it? That is by no means a coincidence. These are two clever examples of how online behavior designers make undesirable behavior more difficult.

So far, this section has been about how we can facilitate the desired behavior. But sometimes it is better to do the opposite: make the unwanted behavior more difficult. This is because the Fogg Behavior Model works both ways: the chance of achieving the desired behavior increases if we make it easier, but decreases if we make it more difficult. Take a look at how it's done below. It is a lot easier to confirm here than to close the window.

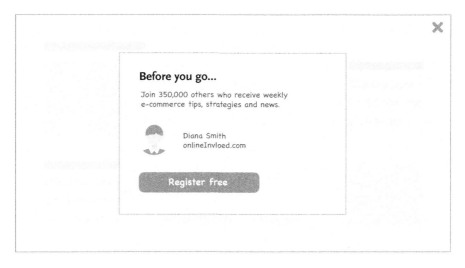

In everyday life, we constantly make it difficult to do unwanted behavior. Take the urinal in a men's toilet, for example: it's usually impossible to set down your half-full beer glass anywhere. As a result, men are more likely to do the desired behavior: they do not take their glasses to the men's room.

Another example can be found on well-designed menus. Restaurant owners prefer guests to choose a dish based on their taste, not their wallet. That is why the cost of dishes is almost never ranked from low to high, but jumbled up. This makes undesirable behavior, making a choice based on price, a lot more difficult.

Online applications

The same happens in online environments. We have plenty of good examples, but also many not so good ones. To clarify this range, we have divided it into three categories: noble, neutral and questionable applications.

Noble applications – everyone benefits

- Asking users to enter their email address twice makes it more difficult to get it wrong.
- Automatically shutting down addictive apps after an hour of play, makes it harder to continue.

Neutral applications – a little guidance, as part of the persuasion process

- By leaving out the navigation buttons in the checkout of a web shop, it is more difficult to continue shopping at that stage.
- Making the button with the negative option smaller than the button with the positive option makes it more difficult to click on the negative.

Questionable applications – going too far by making people desperate

- By ticking the 'Take out travel insurance' option by default, it is more difficult not to take out travel insurance when purchasing a flight ticket.
- Requiring Facebook users to select a reason to unsubscribe from a long list, makes it more difficult to delete an account.

This brings us to a condition in the application of this principle. We believe that you should only make behavior more difficult if it is also undesirable to your visitors to a certain extent.

What is the undesirable behavior?

As an online behavior designer, you are constantly thinking about what you want your visitors to do. Conversely, it is also wise to consider what you do not want them to do. What is the undesirable behavior? And how can you prevent your visitors behaving in this way? If an option is undesirable for you and your visitors alike, you have to make it a difficult option.

 Make behavior that is undesirable for you and/or your visitors extra difficult

What should you remember?

- We are a little more likely to give up when things get difficult.
- You can sometimes increase the chances of the desired behavior happening by making the undesirable behavior more difficult.

What can you do?

- Make behavior that is undesirable for you or your visitors extra difficult.
- Therefore, define all the behaviors that you prefer your visitors not to do.
- See if you can make that behavior more difficult in a reasonable and ethical way.

Part 5
How to design choices

HOW TO DESIGN CHOICES
What is choice architecture?

In the *Ability* chapter, you read that with the default technique we not only make choice behavior easier, we can actually guide it. As behavior designers, we also have other strategies in our toolbox to influence choices besides the default technique. How we present our options plays an important part here. This is why we call it 'choice architecture'.

Earlier in this book, we already drew a comparison between our profession and that of architects. Just like an architect uses physical principles to design a building, so you can use psychological principles to design a choice or choice set. We will cover five principles you can use for this:

Hobson + 1
Consider offering a second option in addition to the desired behavior.

Anchoring
Make sure your value feels higher or lower by working with contrasting values right before or nearby.

Extreme aversion
If applicable, add any 'extreme' options to both sides of a choice set.

Decoy
Add an 'ugly brother' to your choice set to show how attractive the choice you want them to pick is; follow your own moral compass.

Nudging

Give your visitors a subtle nudge in the direction of one or two options that you want them to choose.

If you apply these principles carefully, your visitors are more likely to display the behavior you want. One side note: you can use this mainly when your visitors do not really have a strong preference. In other words, you help them choose.

If we're only offered one option, we also consider the 'do nothing' option

HOW TO DESIGN CHOICES
Hobson + 1

Thomas Hobson had a courier company and delivered mail between Cambridge and London. If his horses were not busy, he would rent them out to students. When people arrived at his extensive stables, there were dozens of horses to choose from. At least, that's what people thought ... Hobson had one golden rule: customers could only choose the horse in the stall closest to the door. What would you do? Go on foot or hire that one horse anyway?

Many of Hobson's customers chose the latter, to the delight of Hobson, who prevented his best and fastest horses from always being chosen. What he was really saying to his clients, was: "Take it or leave it." A 'Hobson's choice' is still a well-known English expression for a 'free' choice that is more or less forced upon you.

It may have been a brilliant move at the time, but offering a single option online is not always the best solution. For your visitors, 'doing nothing' is often also an option worth considering. Especially since it takes only a few clicks to go to the next web shop. Today's customers don't have to walk for hours to the next horse livery, either.

This is why it can be helpful to add a second option to your default option. This shifts the attention to the choice between those two particular options, and steers the focus away from the 'do nothing' option. This principle is known as Hobson + 1, a term coined by Bart Schutz, a Dutch consumer psychologist.[33]

Shift of choice

You can apply the Hobson + 1 principle in many online environments, because there are always certain behaviors that you want to encourage your visitors to perform: confirm, order, download, log in, get in touch, and so on. It is usually possible to add a second option.

We did this, for example, in an email that kicked off a customer satisfaction survey of a Dutch bank: Adding that extra option doubled the conversion for 'Yes, I want to help'.

👍 **Do**
Offer a secondary choice so that the option of 'doing nothing' is emphasized less.

👎 **Don't**
Offer only one option.

Searching for choices

So, your task is simple. Find all the singular choices that your visitors encounter during their customer journey and try to add a second option. Then, test whether conversion has improved.

A few examples for inspiration:

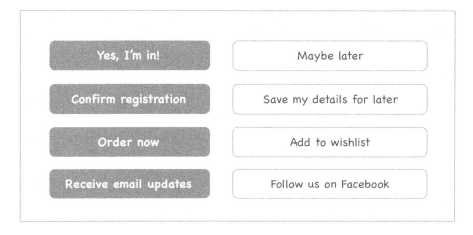

Finally, three practical tips. Offer the two options close together so that your visitors see them together and consider them together. If you position them too far apart, the option of 'doing nothing' may still come into the picture. Make sure the two options also fit together in terms of content, for example 'Yes, I'm in' and 'Maybe later'. If they do not match, 'doing nothing' may still be the alternative. And finally: give the desired option more visual attention, to make choosing easier.

ONLY ONE ADDITIONAL OPTION
Why only one additional option, and not two, three or four? Because with multiple options your visitors may be afraid to make the 'wrong' choice, and miss out on something as a consequence. Doubt slows customers down. That is why it is best to start by trying one additional option.

 Consider offering a second option in addition to the desired behavior

What should you remember?

- If we're only offered one option, we also consider the 'do nothing' option.
- But if we are presented with two options, we shift our attention to the choice between those two options, and the 'do nothing' option is given less emphasis.
- We call this the 'Hobson + 1 principle'.

What can you do?

- Consider offering a second option in addition to the desired behavior.
- Offer these two options close to one another and make sure they match in content.
- Give the second option less visual emphasis than the first.

When evaluating values we are influenced by the value of things that are nearby or which we have seen just before

HOW TO DESIGN CHOICES
Anchoring

When Steve Jobs introduced the iPad in 2010, everyone expected him to tell them what the device would cost. He kept it to himself until the end of his presentation. However, in the run-up, he displayed a 'random' amount on the huge screen behind him for half an hour: $ 999. When Jobs announced the actual prices, the room breathed a collective sigh of relief. The cheapest iPad turned out to be only $ 499 and the most expensive only $ 829.

Steve gets his audience used to a high amount (anchor).

As a result, prices shown afterwards are perceived as cheaper.

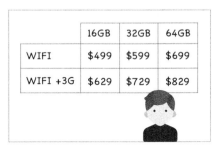

Jobs made clever use of what we refer to as 'anchoring' in psychology. He exposed the room to an expectation, the 'anchor', after which the final – still high – amount was better than expected.

Dan Ariely demonstrated this in a well-known experiment.[34] He asked his students to estimate the value of several products, for example, a bottle of wine. But first, he asked them to write down the last two digits of their social security number. He then asked if they would be happy to pay that amount in dollars for the bottle of wine. The students thought it was an odd question, since they knew this was a completely random amount. But Ariely had worked this out very cleverly. He wanted to know if the height of this random number could influence the valuation. Finally, he asked the students to make a bid on the wine. And yes, he did find a significant effect. The students who had written down a high number, for example $ 89) made a much higher bid than those who had written down a low number (for example, $ 11). They offered up to three times as much.

If System 1 has to assess whether something is expensive or cheap, it allows itself to be influenced by random numbers around it. If you see a higher number first, followed by a price that is lower, your subconscious thinks that price is not too bad. If you see a lower number first, you will unconsciously think: that is expensive. This effect mainly occurs if you do not really have a clear idea of how much something should cost.

In the world of marketing and sales, anchoring is not exactly a new phenomenon. Take the sellers in North African medinas, for example. They price their wares so ridiculously high that you're extremely proud if you haggle 50 percent off – and still end up paying too much for it.

In practice

As an online designer, you can also use the Anchoring principle, by examining the moments in the customer journey where you can offer a contrast to influence the perception of the desired choice option. A few examples for inspiration:

- If you prefer to sell the medium version of a product, show your visitors the most expensive version first by presenting it in front.

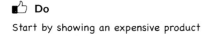

Do
Start by showing an expensive product

Don't
Show your cheapest product first

- If you want to make prices appear lower, use 'from/for prices'.

Manufacturer's suggested retail price $ 39.99

31.35

- If you want to emphasize your excellent customer satisfaction ratio, put your worst-performing competitor first in the comparison list.

Compare customer satisfaction

Competitor 1	5.4	★★★★★½
You	8.5	★★★★★★★★½
Competitor 2	8.2	★★★★★★★★½

 Make sure your value feels higher or lower by working with contrasting values before or nearby

What should you remember?

- When evaluating values, we are influenced by the value of things that are nearby or which we have seen just before.
- We call this the 'Anchoring principle'.

What can you do?

- Make sure your value feels higher or lower by working with contrasting values right before or nearby.
- If you want to make something appear lower, smaller or less, contrast it with something higher, larger or more.
- If you want to make something appear higher, larger or more, contrast it with something lower, smaller, or less.

We don't like to choose 'extremes'

HOW TO DESIGN CHOICES

Extreme aversion

You're on your way to a meeting. You are in a hurry, but you still have to eat something. Which portion size of French fries do you order when you get to the drive-through of the fast food chain: small, medium or extra large?

Chances are that you will go for the middle option. This is because we don't like to choose 'extremes, even when it's just the first and last option in a set of choices. This is evident from a series of studies by marketing scientist Itamar Simonson and psychologist Amos Tversky.[35] Their conclusion: in an option set, we find an option more attractive if it is the intermediate option. And vice versa: we find the options on the outside, so the first and the last, less attractive.

We do not like to choose the outer options.
As a result, these are chosen less often.

Why is that? Probably because in life, 'extreme' usually stands for risky. And in our urge to survive, we have traditionally been inclined to avoid risks. That is why in psychology we call it the 'Extreme Aversion principle'.

Adding options

This principle can help you when you design a choice process. In the following example, the best-selling option, 'Basic', is shown on the left. Due to extreme aversion, you may just miss out on conversion as a result.

What you could do is show an additional option on the left, like the free trial version you were offering anyway. As a result, 'Basic' shifts to the middle and this option feels less 'extreme'.

 Add additional 'extreme' options to both sides of a choice set, if you can offer them

What should you remember?

- We don't like to choose 'extremes'.
- This also applies to the first and last option in a choice set.
- We call this the 'Extreme Aversion principle'.

What can you do?

- Check if the option you are aiming for is on the outside of the choice set (far left or far right).
- If that is the case, position additional 'extreme' options on the sides if you have them.

We find an option more attractive if its 'ugly brother' is standing next to it

HOW TO DESIGN CHOICES
Decoy

Suppose you want to give young start-ups a chance and you go to Kickstarter, a well-known website for crowdfunding. Which offer do you choose? Invest ten dollars and receive an e-book? Or invest 20 dollars and receive both an e-book and a hardcover? Most people chose the cheapest option: only the e-book.

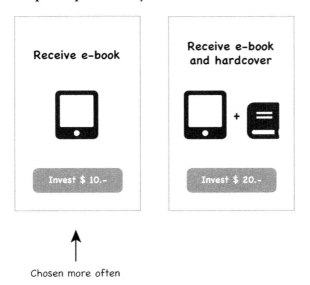

Chosen more often

This choice from two options comes from a study at the University of Liechtenstein.[36] The researchers wondered what would happen if they added a third option: an option that was just as expensive as the most expensive option, but clearly less attractive (a 'decoy'). The new choice set looked as follows:

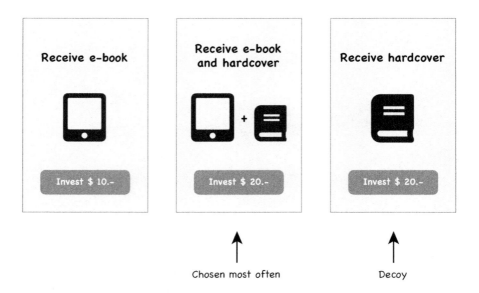

The result? Suddenly, the least popular option (e-book and hardcover) had become the most popular. The researchers were also able to calculate that sales would increase by 10 percent if they added this unattractive option in real life.

This so-called 'Decoy effect' has been demonstrated in many studies. The decoy is an option that looks suspiciously like the target option, but is clearly less attractive. So, the decoy makes the target option more attractive. We also call the decoy the 'ugly brother' (see box).

UGLY BROTHER?

Dan Ariely, an Israeli-American professor of psychology and behavioral economics, has done a lot of research into decoys. In one of his experiments, he compared the attractiveness of Tom and Jerry.[37] If Tom's ugly brother was shown next to Tom, the participants thought Tom was more attractive than Jerry. But if Jerry's ugly brother was shown next to Jerry, they thought Jerry was more handsome.

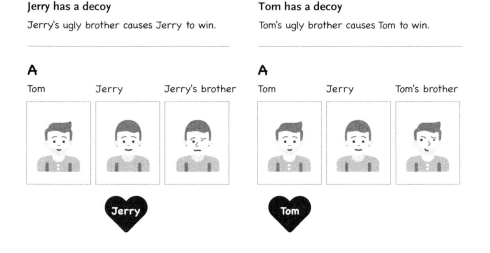

Practical

If you are designing a product range, price table or subscription structure, you can always use the Decoy principle. The ugly brother should look very much like the handsome brother, but just a bit 'less' so, and so much so that the ugly brother himself will most likely not be chosen. There is a side note: you have to be able to deliver the ugly brother if your visitors ask for it. Fun fact: in the Kickstarter experiment, four test persons chose the decoy.

Ethical

For some people, the Decoy principle feels like deception because the decoy is added purely to influence people. You could also see it like this, however: the ugly brother really shows your visitors the value of the handsome brother. In our opinion, it is a borderline case. In any case, no information is deliberately hidden.

 Add an 'ugly brother' to your choice set to show how attractive the choice you want is, while following your own moral compass

What should you remember?

- We find an option more attractive if the 'ugly brother' is positioned next to it.

What can you do?

- Add an 'ugly brother' to your choice set to show how attractive the choice you want is.
- follow your moral compass.
- The ugly brother should look very much like the handsome brother, but just a bit 'less' so, and so much so that the ugly brother himself will most likely not be chosen.
- You should make sure, however, that you are able to deliver the ugly brother.

We sometimes need a little nudge to be able to make a choice

HOW TO DESIGN CHOICES

Nudging

Have you ever bought a laptop online? Then you have probably seen how incredibly wide the range is. And how difficult it often is to choose between all those products that look so similar to each other. How wonderful is it, then, to get a nudge in the right direction?

In psychology, a nudge is defined as a push in the right direction. Currys PC World, for example, does this conveniently with labels that draw attention to specific products. Some examples by Currys and other companies:

- Most popular choice
- Our experts love
- Limited stock deal
- Discounted today only
- Free extension cable

This takes the Nudge principle just one step further than the default principle. (See the *Default, prefill and autocomplete* chapter in part 4). A default is a neutral pre-selection, while a nudge takes things one step further.

Multiple principles

The label is a nudge in and of itself: a product with a label stands out in an environment where other products do not have a label. However, you can guide even more with the text on your label. We have applied a variety of principles in these texts in the list above:

- *Most popular choice* — Social proof
- *Bestseller* — Social proof
- *Tested as best by the Consumer Association* — Authority
- *Only three left in stock* — Scarcity in stock
- *Discounted today only* — Scarcity in time
- *Free extension cable* — Simply a great offer

You are giving your visitors a good reason to make a certain choice. We also call this the 'visual variant' of the Reasons Why principle. (See the *Reasons Why* chapter in Part 3.) You can only find out which variant works best by comparing two different stickers in an A/B test.

Finally: add a nudge to one or two options only. If you add a nudge to more options, you will only create choice stress.

The advice
Give your visitors a subtle nudge in the direction of one or two options that you want them to choose

What should you remember?

- We sometimes need a little nudge to be able to make a choice.

What can you do?

- Give your visitors a subtle nudge in the direction of one or two options that you want them to choose.

Part 6

How to apply behavioral psychology

And now: how to put it all into practice

You now know that online behavior – like any other behavior – only happens after a strong prompt, sufficient motivation and sufficient ability. Moreover, you now know the most important principles you can use to influence these three factors. This allows you to tackle virtually any conversion challenge, at least if you know which strategy to use where and when. In other words: it's high time to dive into practice.

In the remainder of this book, we will examine several online applications: online ads, email ads, search engine ads, landing pages, product pages and checkouts. For each of these so-called touch points, we will give you concrete guidelines based on the theory we have discussed. This will help you not only to *understand* how the principles work, but also to *apply* them in a targeted way.

HOW TO APPLY BEHAVIORAL PSYCHOLOGY
Online advertising

Online behavior often starts with a click on an online ad. And a good start is half the job, as they say. Based on the design principles in the previous chapters, we can make these ads more effective than by randomly brainstorming without scientific knowledge or just copying what others do.

On the following pages, we will show you in detail how to apply these design principles to the two most common online ads: display ads (on websites) and ads on social media. But first, we need to manage your expectations.

Online advertising is a form of interruption marketing. In other words: you are approaching someone who is actually doing something else at that moment, for example, planning a bicycle route, browsing pictures of their favorite artist, or reading the news. Nobody likes to be distracted during these activities. So, be aware that the vast majority of your target audience will ignore your ad.

Recently, one of our novice behavior designers was at her wits' end. Why, you ask? Only 0.1 percent of visitors had clicked on her banner. When we told her that the worldwide average for this type of ad is 0.05 percent, she perked right up. And rightly so, because in reality she did twice as well as the average online marketer.

Banner[38]	Social[39]	Email[40]	Search[41]
0.05 percent	0.9 percent	2.5 percent	2.7 per cent

The average click-through rate for some forms of online advertising.

Design for a 7-year-old

At the start of this book, we explained that our brain works with two systems: System 1 (our automatic brain) and System 2 (the brain that only comes into action when System 1 notices something fun or special). System 1's limited capacity for reading and understanding text is crucial here. That is why we compare System 1 to a 7-year-old child. A 7-year-old mainly scans pictures, reads only short and simple texts, and ignores anything that is too long or too complicated.

Because the target audience of your online ad is, by definition, busy doing something else, you can be sure that your ad will first be perceived by System 1. That is why, as a behavior designer, it is smart to design your ads for that child of 7.

Keep it simple

How do you design ads for that 7-year-old kid? Mainly by keeping things simple. In other words: don't stuff your ad with too much stuff. The aim of an online ad is for people to *click* on it. *Persuasion* comes afterwards.

But what if you work for a large organization, where you often have to deal with managers who want to add all sorts of items to your ad? The 'brand manager' may want to add a company logo or slogan. Or the 'Legal' department may ask you to put in a disclaimer. These factors can make it difficult to keep your ad simple. Hopefully, the arguments in this book will help you to convince other stakeholders.

Clean and simple

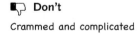

Crammed and complicated

Consider the cost model

We finish off this chapter with the cost model. This is also relevant for the design of your online ad. We distinguish three variants:

- **Cost per click** (CPC). As an advertiser, you pay a fixed amount per click on a display ad (banner) or link. For example: $5 per click on the ad or link.
- **Cost per mille** (CPM). As an advertiser, you pay for a number of ad displays. For example: $1 for a thousand displays of an ad.
- **Cost per action** (CPA). As an advertiser you pay for the desired action. For example: $10 for each visitor who subscribes to your newsletter. This conversion-oriented cost model is also known as 'cost per lead' (CPL) or 'cost per sale' (CPS).

Before you design an ad, you need to carefully consider which cost model applies.

With CPM, it makes little difference whether people outside your target audience click on your ad. As long as they don't perform the desired action – subscribing to the newsletter – you don't pay anything extra for their click on your ad. So, in that case, you have to design an ad that many people will click on.

For CPC, it's a different story. Because with CPC, advertisers pay per click, it is better to design an ad that only tempts your specific target group.

With CPA, it doesn't really matter from your perspective if people outside your target group click on your ad. As long as they don't perform the desired action – subscribing to the newsletter – you don't pay anything for their click on your ad. From the perspective of the person promoting your site, however, it does matter: they want to get the maximum return from the click-throughs to your site. That is why designing an ad that is only tempting for your specific target group is preferable.

In the following chapters, we highlight display ads, social media ads, search engine ads, and email ads. Needless to say, there are other types of ads, but these channels are the most popular. We also include the cost model in this.

HOW TO APPLY BEHAVIORAL PSYCHOLOGY
Display ads

By display advertising, we mean banners. Most people hate them, but they're everywhere. It's hardly surprising, because banners are still a good way to earn money with online content. A click on a banner can be the first step in a customer journey that ends with a purchase, a download or a subscription to your newsletter.

But did you know that most banner campaigns are loss-making? In other words: the advertising costs are higher than the additional sales that the ads generate. So why do companies often keep opting for display advertising? Because banners also increase brand awareness of your brand or your product, which can generate more sales in the long run. Compare them to advertising boards lining the soccer field.

In this chapter, we do not focus on branding but on generating plenty of response. We'll start with attention and affordance. Next, we will discuss how to apply three prompt strategies to banners (Curiosity, Exceptional benefit and Simple question) and how to make your banner short and powerful with the Jenga technique.

Grab attention
Understand that banners are, first and foremost, a prompt: they should tempt your target group to a first click. This means that above all, they should attract attention.

Banner blindness
Moreover, our brain has taught itself over time to ignore banners. That is: banners that look like banners. We call this 'banner blindness'. This may sound like a handicap, but it is, in fact, a useful skill.

So how can you attract attention? Our most favorable method is the use of subtle movements. The transition from static to moving is almost impossible to ignore. In the *Attention* chapter in Part 2, you can find more tips on how to attract attention to your banner.

Another strategy to circumvent banner blindness is to design your banner in such a way that it resembles the content of the website itself (also known as 'native advertising'). In that case, it would be reasonable to indicate that the message is sponsored.

Use videos that tell a story
Using videos in banners can work well. After all: movement attracts attention. To retain your target group's attention, something meaningful should happen in your video. Atmospheric videos without clear meaning have less of an impact than videos that tell a mini story. For example, demonstrate that a shirt is water-repellent by splashing water on it. Or when promoting a new car: fill up the trunk space with lots of stuff.

Advertisement as a pop-up
Banners that appear as pop-ups in your central vision are the most notorious example of interrupt marketing. By definition, these banners grab all the attention. So, you don't have to use any strategies in the design to draw attention away. However, do choose a good prompt strategy, so that the visitor does not click the ad shut too quickly. Elsewhere in this chapter, we will tell you more about this.

Design affordance
In the *Affordance* chapter in Part 2, you read that a prompt absolutely requires good affordance. It is a bit of a miracle that you even attract attention – and then people should immediately understand that they can click and know where to click.

Your banner must primarily contain a recognizable button shape. System 1 should understand in a millisecond that your banner is clickable. The good old 'Click here' button still works wonders:

Incidentally, it doesn't always have to be a button per se. Playback buttons, checkboxes and arrow shapes are also excellent options, provided they are clearly *clickable*.

The Curiosity strategy

One way to entice people to a click, is to make them curious. Exactly how you do that depends on the underlying cost model. That is why we provide practical advice and an example for each cost model.

CPM: *focus on making people curious*

With CPM, advertisers pay for the number of *displays* of the ad. For you as a designer, this means it is less important who clicks on it; as long as it's a lot of people. It doesn't matter if a person who clicks falls outside your target group, because you've already paid for the display anyway. In other words, you can focus all your efforts on curiosity. The examples below inspire maximum curiosity, because you are not yet revealing your offer:

CPC: *arouse curiosity and filter*

With CPC, advertisers pay a fixed amount for each click. In that case, as a designer, you have to make sure that only your target group clicks on the banner. If you do this purely based on curiosity, things could go south pretty fast. Take a look at this banner, for example:

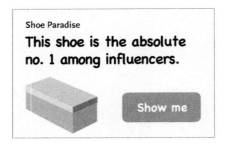

This banner is likely to result in more clicks, but many of these people probably don't want to buy shoes at all; they only click because they are interested in celebrities' tastes in shoes. As a result, you are robbing your own purse, because you have to pay a fixed amount for every person who clicks.

In this case, it is smart to make people curious, but also to filter immediately, as with this variant:

Generates less curiosity? Maybe so. But it still makes some people interested. And you know for sure that you waste virtually no advertising budget on people who just want to find out more about celebrities.

CPA: arouse curiosity and filter
With CPA, advertisers pay for the desired action. You may think that it doesn't matter who clicks on your banner, because you or your client only pays for conversion when there is conversion. But make no mistake: operators of advertising space are not stupid. If too many people who click don't convert, they would rather replace it with a different banner or raise the price per conversion.

This is why for CPA, the same applies as for CPC: use curiosity, but also filter by target group. All you want here are clicks from people you can actually tempt during the remainder of the customer journey.

Make people curious with text and visuals
In the examples above, you have seen that you can easily make people curious with text. Visuals are another good way to do so; for example, by covering something partially or completely, you can easily tempt people to click:

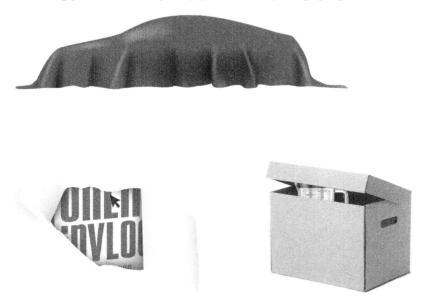

The Exceptional-benefit strategy
Earlier on, you read that we are quick to drop our task if there is an exceptional benefit to be gained. The Exceptional-benefit strategy is, therefore, nicely suited for banners. The underlying cost model plays less of a role here, because only interested audiences will click on it.

The following applies to this technique: formulate it simply and concretely. System 1 should immediately understand the benefit and activate System 2 on that basis:

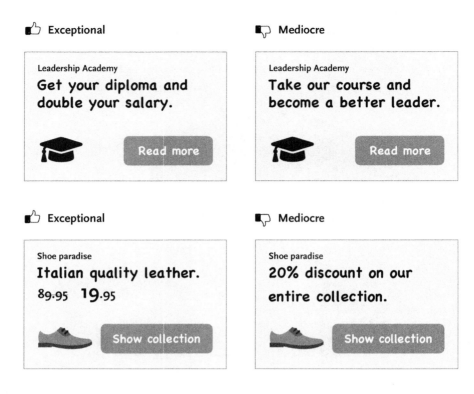

You probably won't win the originality award with banners like this. But the aim of this book is not to make design all about creativity. It is all about behavior, so exceptional benefit, in all its simplicity, is an excellent strategy.

CPC: *harder* CTAS

If you pay per click when using the Exceptional-benefit strategy, use harder calls to action. You will probably generate fewer clicks, but the willingness to buy in the people who click is higher:

Soft CTA: more clicks, poorer traffic	Hard CTA: fewer clicks, better traffic
Discover the benefits	Become a member
Check our promotion	Order today
Explore	Sign up

The Simple-question strategy

As described in *Part 2: How to Design Winning Prompts,* a simple question can pull us away from what we are busy doing. You can take advantage of this premise when designing your banner. All you have to do is come up with a simple question and have multiple answer buttons.

The buttons must link to different variants of a landing page because your visitors expect a response that matches the answer they clicked on:

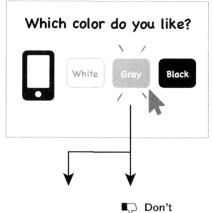

 Do
Specific landing page that matches the choice made in the banner.

 Don't
General landing page that does not match the choice made in the banner.

With some types of banners, it is not possible to link each button to its own URL. In that case, you can still show different buttons in your banner, with different texts, which refer in a natural way to the same landing page. The example below illustrates this:

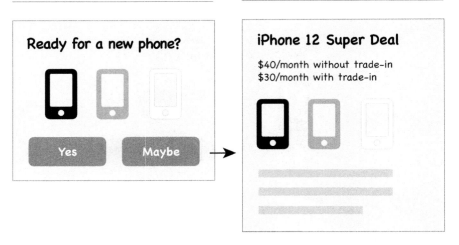

No matter which button you click, the transition to the general landing page is perceived as logical.

The Jenga technique

The fewer words you use, the easier it is for our automatic brain to read and understand the text. Skillfully remove superfluous words from your banner with the Jenga technique and use only simple words, preferably colloquial language. If you use five words or less, chances are that your target audience reads the text automatically and not even consciously. (See *The Jenga Technique* chapter in part 4.) In the example, you can see how we have reduced fifteen words to six, without losing the essence. One of the reasons we decided not to mention 'The Mindfulness Institute' as the sender, was because it is not a well-known brand. We can announce the fact that you have to register first (for the newsletter) later, on the landing page.

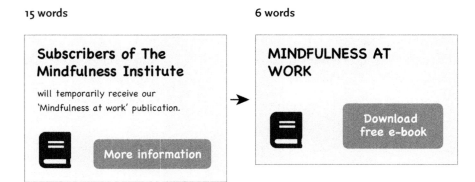

Thankless job?

Designing display ads sometimes feels a bit like a thankless job. After all, your ad has to compete with endless other ads. In addition, banner blindness makes people increasingly skilled at ignoring banners. Fortunately, you are now armed with the design principles that you can use in display advertising. If you apply them smartly, your prompt will beat those of all the other designers.

HOW TO APPLY BEHAVIORAL PSYCHOLOGY
Social media ads

We spend an average of two hours a day on social media. It is, therefore, not surprising that advertisers try to reach their target groups via, among others, Facebook, Instagram and LinkedIn. In this chapter, you will discover which design strategies can take your social media advertising to the next level.

For the sake of clarity: this chapter is not about influencers who regularly feature products in their posts. By social media advertising, we mean designing sponsored messages that appear on the timelines of your target audience. The main advantage of this form of advertising is that you can come to the attention of a specific target group, for example, highly educated women between 30 and 40 years of age who like to travel and live in New York. Or with skilled male workers between 15 and 25 years of age who love fast cars and live in the Mid-West.

If you apply this segmentation at the front, the average click ratio on social media is much higher than for display advertising. On average, 0.5 percent of all users click through: one in two hundred.

Attention and stopping power
When you scroll through your timeline on social media, a lot of ads appear on your screen in between the posts of your friends and colleagues. And whether you like it or not, you have to scroll past them. Social media users often exhibit this behavior at a rapid pace. That's why the main aim of your ads should be to grab people's attention and to persuade them to click and move away from their timeline.

Movement draws the most attention. That is why video ads are generally a lot more effective than their text-based counterparts. Videos with a mini story have particularly effective stopping power. Take the following ad by Samsung, for example. It shows a painting that slowly morphs into a television. This striking transition makes it virtually impossible not to look:

A practical tip to attract the attention of your specific target group: take a look at some timelines of people who belong to your target group. By designing content that blends in nicely in their timelines, you increase the chance that they won't just scroll past your ad.

BEWARE OF ADVERTISEMENT BLINDNESS
Social media users want to be entertained. That's why beautiful, cute or funny pictures always work well. At least: if they are real photographs, because System 1 has developed a blind spot for clichéd stock images. Advertising blindness, therefore, also plays a role in social media advertising. Large logos and excessively promotional texts should also be avoided.

Just as with display advertising, the Curiosity strategy, the Exceptional-benefit strategy, and the Simple-question strategy are ways to design your social media ad as an effective prompt. We'll deal with them one by one.

The Curiosity strategy

Generating curiosity is also an excellent way to generate clicks on social media. And just as with display advertising, you should carefully consider the underlying cost model.

CPM: arouse curiosity

If, as an advertiser, you pay for the *number of displays* (CPM), you have nothing to worry about. Your only goal is to design an ad that makes people curious and invites many people to click on it. The next ad, which eventually calls for donations, is a good example of this:

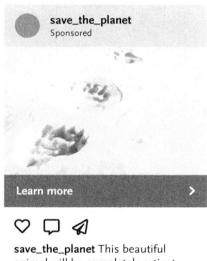

CPC and CPA: arouse curiosity and filter

If, as an advertiser, you pay *per click* (CPC) or *per action* (CPA), it is wiser to make it clear right away that it is a donation. In other words: you should filter out anyone who would never donate. You can do this, for example, with your caption under the photo, but also with a more specific call to action. Your ad will probably generate fewer clicks, but that is exactly your intention. After all, the clicks you do get will be from people who know that the idea is to donate and are not put off by that. A higher chance of conversion, in other words.

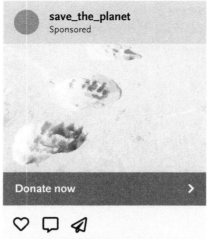

You can also make the Curiosity principle work for you by consciously showing products *without* the corresponding price. Out of curiosity, many people will click on the ad to find out the price. Once they've done that, they've taken the first baby step in their customer journey and they will be more open to further persuasion:

Not showing price
Arouses curiosity.

Showing price
Arouses less curiosity.

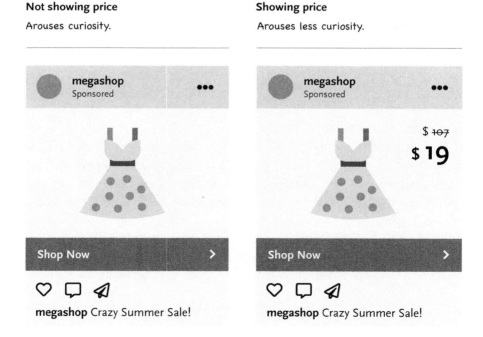

The Exceptional-benefit strategy

We are also sensitive to exceptional benefits while we are using social media. Expensive, beautiful or special products for a remarkably low price or with a high discount, therefore, invite you to click. We have already indicated that with display advertising, too much text causes System 1, similar to a 7-year-old child, to automatically ignore the ad. Therefore, in social media ads, stick to short and powerful words to communicate your benefit.

Just like social media users, you can put a text under your post as an advertiser. Make use of this option, because ads with a text at the bottom usually score better. It also helps to keep your ad 'clean', because you can put some of the text somewhere else. Take a look at the difference between the two ads below:

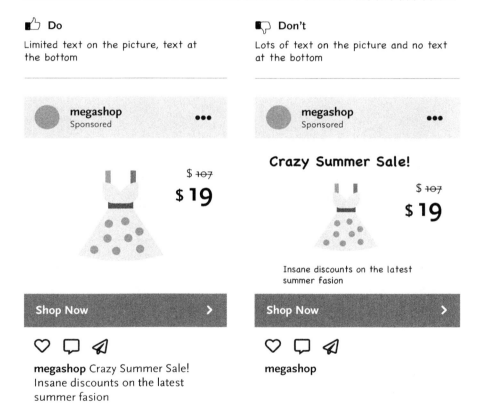

The Simple-question strategy

The Simple-question strategy is also an effective approach to social media advertising, albeit a little more difficult to apply here than display advertising. For social media, it is not yet possible to work with more than one answer button. In addition, it is usually not possible to write the text for your buttons yourself.

Still, there is a way to apply this strategy to social media advertising, i.e. by suggesting that there are several buttons:

Because the buttons are not real, your visitors always land on the same landing page. But what matters is that you make them think about the answer to the question you ask. In doing so, you pull them away from their timeline. And that brings them one step closer to conversion.

After the click
Social media apps have ensured that the landing page is loaded into their app, so that visitors can return to their ever-so-interesting timeline with one click on the 'back button'.

This is why 'soft conversions' are the most successful, whereby you don't immediately ask for a lot of data, or a significant commitment such as a purchase. (See the *Baby Steps* chapter in Part 3.) For example, ask only for someone's email so that you have the opportunity to follow up later.

You can also use so-called 'lead ads', whereby the form to be completed is part of the social media app, such as Facebook. The advantage is that you can complete the form quickly and that, for example, your name and email address have already been entered in advance. The disadvantage is that, as a behavior designer, you do not have much influence on the design of the form:

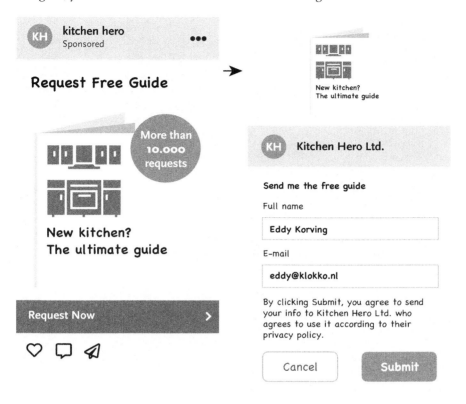

Here, again, don't ask too many questions. The more questions, the more visitors drop out, especially when you ask for their phone number.

This is hardly surprising because this feels like private information and, therefore, a significant commitment. Good to know: research indicates that if you ask for both a phone number and email address, you will have more success than if you only ask for the phone number. (See table.[42]) Possible explanation: with the latter option it feels as if you will definitely be called.

	Conversion ratio	Cost per lead
Only ask for email address	33.8 percent	$ 1.38
Only ask for telephone number	15.3 percent	$ 6.09
Ask for email address and telephone number	18.6 percent	$ 4.38

HOW TO APPLY BEHAVIORAL PSYCHOLOGY
Email ads

With email ads you reach your target group very directly. Whether you compile the recipient list yourself or buy it somewhere, potential customers receive your email directly in their mailbox. But that doesn't mean they'll open it, let alone click through to your landing page and convert there. Fortunately, you can increase that chance with good behavior design.

You have to make sure that recipients do the following:

- open the email;
- in the email, click through to a landing page;
- proceed to the desired behavior on the landing page.

To get recipients to open your mail, you design a catchy subject line, because that will increase the so-called 'open rate' (OR): the percentage of recipients that actually open the email. Once the recipients have opened your email, you want them to click through to your landing page. If that happens, the click through rate (CTR) increases: the percentage of recipients that click through. And then there's the click-to-open rate (CTO): the percentage of openers that click through.

However, opening and clicking are only the first steps: the ultimate aim is conversion. For example, you want the recipient of your email to buy something, sign up for your newsletter, or download your white paper. We're talking about the final conversion ratio of your email campaign: the number of conversions as a percentage of the number of recipients of the email.

Make your subject line stand out visually

We can't say it often enough: every behavior starts with attention to your prompt. The same applies to email ads. Take a look at the screenshot of Joris' mailbox, in which you encounter all manner of things:

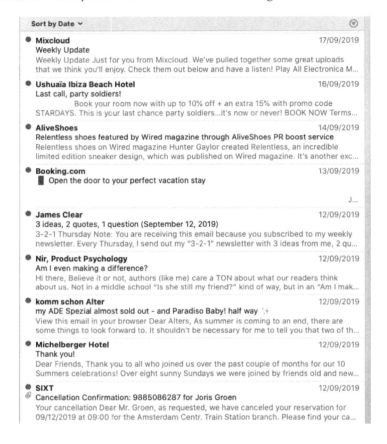

Which subject line immediately catches the eye? The one from Booking.com. It's not so much the content, but because it stands out visually thanks to the eye-catching icon and the empty white line. Deviating from the environment is, therefore, a simple but smart way to attract attention. (See the *Attention* chapter in Part 2.)

Address people personally in the subject line

If recipients see their own name, a subject line is more likely to stand out. That is why we often measure a higher open rate when we personally address someone, as in this example:

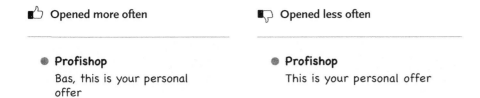

Psychologists also call this the 'Cocktail-party effect'. When everyone is talking at a party, it is almost impossible to hear what everyone is saying. But if someone calls your name on the other side of the room, you'll hear it over all the noise. That's because System 1 analyzes all the sounds around you and only alerts System 2 when something might be important. And that could just apply to hearing your name.

A person as the sender

The name of the sender of the email is always displayed in combination with the subject line. An email from a person has greater appeal than an email from a brand. However, an unknown person may arouse suspicion. If you combine an unknown person with a known brand, you have a chance of a higher open rate than if you only use a brand name as the sender:

The Exceptional-benefit strategy

You can use the Exceptional-benefit strategy to tempt the recipient to open. But you can only use that strategy if you really have something special to offer. In the example below, the subject line on the right is a little too general, while the subject line on the left feels like an exceptional advantage:

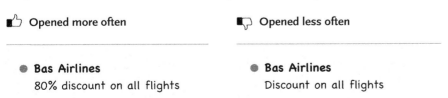

The phrasing of the advantage is often overly complicated. Compare the subject lines below. A 7-year-old will not get the sentence on the right, while the one on the left immediately activates System 2. Formulate your exceptional benefit in plain language:

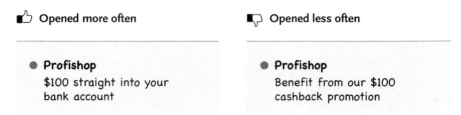

The Curiosity strategy

If you don't have something exceptional to offer, the Curiosity strategy is an excellent approach for your subject line. By using a signal word like 'this', you automatically arouse curiosity:

- This is ...
- Here is ...
- This is how to ...
- This is how you can ...
- In this picture ... (The word 'picture' always scores well.)
- This is the person who... (Recipients want to know who's doing something.)
- This is why...

In the following example on the right, System 1 only thinks: ok great, let's do it, thanks. Yet it feels no reason to open the email, while with the left-hand example it thinks: hold on, let's open it, I wonder what it says?

Research and experience show that asking a question in the subject line makes us less curious than using a signal word. The question may trigger you, but it does not trigger you to open the email:

The Zeigarnik effect

An unfinished task will keep your brain occupied: the Zeigarnik effect. (See the chapter *Unfinished journey* in Part 2.) The subject line of an email is perfect for this purpose. Just compare these two subject lines of an email that should encourage the recipient to write a review:

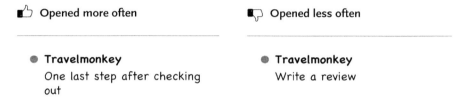

On the right, nothing special is going on. On the left, however, the message is framed as an unfinished task. As a result, recipients are more likely to open the email.

In the following, more or less the same happens as in the previous example. The subject line on the right does nothing special, but the subject line on the left indicates an unfinished task:

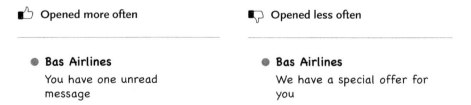

The Bizarreness effect

Are you creative? And do you have a healthy dose of bravado? Then you can design a subject line with a high opening rate based on the Bizarreness effect. For example, like this:

👍 Opened more often   👎 Opened less often

● **British Airways**   ● **Packyourbags.com**
Holy moly!   Holy moly!

'Holy moly!' is a bizarre subject line for British Airways. Attention guaranteed. But beware: this only works if your recipients are familiar with the name of the sender. In combination with an unknown or unreliable sender, people will often see such email as spam.

SUPERLATIVES
Some marketers think that superlatives improve a subject line. However, because superlatives are often associated with advertising, it is actually better to leave them out. Which of the two emails below are you more likely to open?

👍 Opened more often   👎 Opened less often

● **The Whitegoods Store**   ● **The Whitegoods Store**
This is our best promotion   Mega discounts and ultimate
ever   special deals

The content of your email

A strong subject line encourages recipients to open your email. But it takes more than just opening because you also want them to click through to your landing page. So, the content of your email should also attract attention.

If your recipients open an email, there's a good chance you haven't grabbed their full concentration and attention yet. So, the persuasion process starts again from scratch here. This means you have to rethink a smart prompt strategy. It may well be a different strategy than the one you used for your subject line, but before we give examples of this, we will first discuss which formats you can best use for the content of your email. We will discuss three: a single call to action, the list of items, and the personal message.

Format 1: a single call to action
With this format, you try to get the people who open your email to click on something quickly. For example, if it would be to your advantage to guide them quickly from the distracting email program to your landing page.

You do this by addressing System 1 directly. Think of a simple text, a strong visual, and an unmistakable button within the field of vision. The more text, the less likely the people opening your email are to read it. You can compare this format with the design of banners in the chapter on online advertising. Take a look at this email:

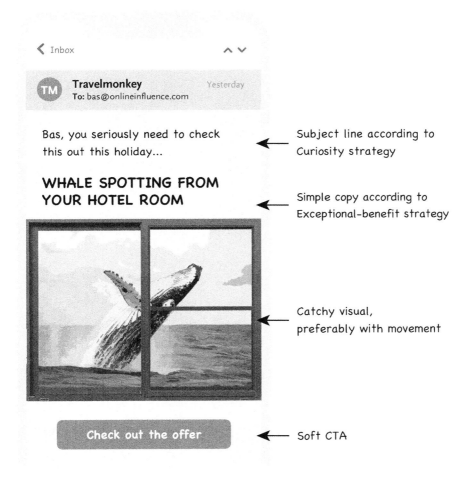

Format 2: the list of items
Another successful format is the list of items. Such a list starts with a title that triggers scrolling and clearly indicates what the list consists of. And if you want to go all out, think of a title that also makes your recipients curious.

Without a title, your list of items doesn't stand a chance. In that case, people who open your email have to make a mental effort to find out what they are looking at. And by now, you are well aware that less mental effort is preferable. A few examples of good titles for your list of items:

- Checklist
- Our best-selling products
- The latest news
- The most read articles in October
- Editor's choice

Next, it is time for step two: designing a list of different blocks. Each individual block is a prompt. So, apply a prompt strategy and a clear call to action for each individual block. Also, design a clear visual rhythm so that the structure of your email is easy to understand, for example, by making it clear where one block ends and the next block begins. An example of a template:

Format 3: a personal message
Finally, let's take a look at the personal message. This format has strong similarities with a personal email, so that the people who open it read it in the same way as an email from a friend or a colleague. Therefore, use a salutation, followed by a short message and a link. Plain and simple, in the standard format, no bells and whistles. Pictures, colors and buttons are not necessary. Don't forget to use a person as the sender:

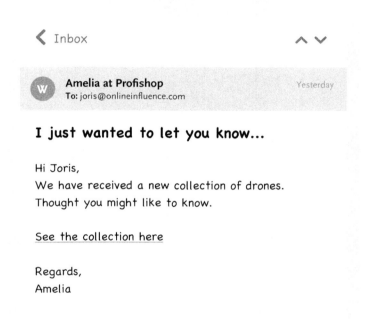

Keep it simple
We will soon be discussing some strategies that will make the content of your email more tempting. But first, we want to highlight one more message: keep it simple. Don't turn your email into a website. Columns and navigation bars, for example, over-complicate your email. In our opinion, they are better left out. The email below is an example of what not to do:

Right, you now have three formats to draw attention with your mail. And you know you have to keep that email simple. It's high time to dive into the three strategies that will definitely tempt the recipients to visit your landing page: Simple question, Exceptional benefit and Curiosity.

The Simple-question strategy

The Simple-question strategy is extremely suitable as a prompt strategy in your email. You probably remember: when we are asked a simple question, we have a strong tendency to answer it. People who open your email often click on one of the answer options if you ask a fun, simple question. This will take them to your landing page, which is exactly what you want. Once there, they are away from all the distracting elements of their mailbox and you can continue to tempt them towards conversion:

Another piece of advice: make sure your visitor lands on a landing page that matches the answer they have given. In other words: the content of the landing page must seamlessly match the answer they gave to your simple question.

The Exceptional-benefit strategy

The Exceptional benefit-strategy also lends itself perfectly to your email. Because recipients have usually consciously opened your mail, you already have some attention from System 2. This means, for example, that you no longer necessarily have to stick to the five-word restriction. The following still applies, however: the more concisely you can articulate the exceptional benefit, the better.

Don't forget to show the benefit in a picture as well. Illustrations that promote the anticipation of a reward are always a good idea. (See the *Anticipatory Enthusiasm* chapter in Part 3.) Please note: only use strong and simple images, and certainly not complicated compilations:

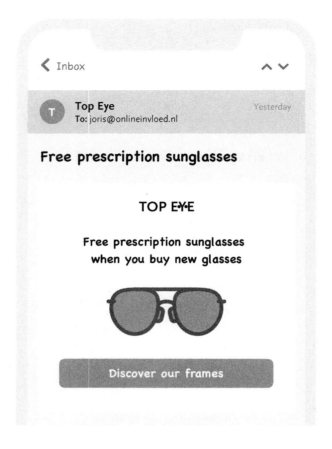

The Curiosity strategy

The Curiosity strategy also works well as a prompt strategy for your email. This already starts in the subject line, but you continue to elaborate on the content of your email by not revealing too much just yet. The real persuasion process, therefore, only starts on the landing page. In this example, you can see how Airbnb uses the Curiosity strategy to tempt users to write a review:

Calls to action in your email

The call to action is a crucial part of every email. To design them to be persuasive, you should take two things into account: ask for small commitments and apply Hobson + 1.

Small commitments

With all forms of advertising, it is best to ask your recipient for small commitments. This also applies to the calls to action in your email. Compare these button texts:

Major commitments: fewer clicks	Small commitments: more clicks
Order now	*Read more*
Buy now	*Check availability*
Sign up	*Register without obligation*
Subscribe	*Check your privileges*
Join	*Discover our promotion*

Hobson + 1

As we mentioned before: adding a second call to action sometimes works wonders. (See the *Baby Steps* chapter in Part 3.) This will change the choice your users have from 'option A versus nothing' to 'option A, option B, or nothing':

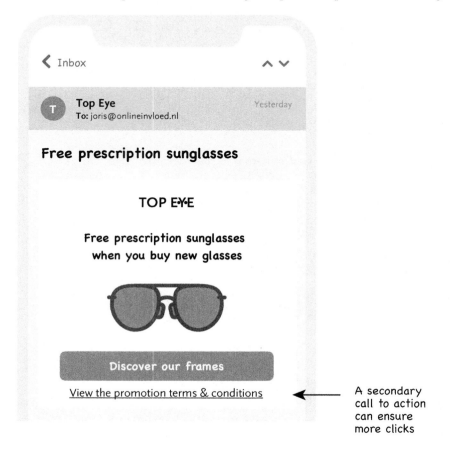

A secondary call to action can ensure more clicks

Animated GIFs

You've probably heard of animated GIFs. An animated GIF is a short animation that does not take up too much bandwidth. You can also use these 'moving pictures' in your emails. A/B tests show that, in some cases, they significantly increase conversion. Let's see if we can explain this with the Fogg Behavior Model.

Prompt

We know that movement attracts attention. You might expect that attracting attention is no longer necessary because your visitor has already opened the email; so there is already enough attention. But on a desktop, the last email people receive usually opens automatically, in other words, without the recipient necessarily paying attention to it. In such cases, attracting attention with movement can be a good idea. In addition, the recipient may be busy doing something else when opening your mail, and, therefore, not give it a hundred percent attention. A moving image at the top of your email increases the chance that the recipient will continue reading.

Ability
The Ability axis shows another reason why an animated GIF may contribute to a higher conversion: an animation can help to explain more clearly what you have to offer. For example, with a GIF you can explain much quicker that you can fold a laptop screen backwards than with a series of static pictures.

Motivation
Finally, animations can contribute to a sense of quality. If you have clearly put a lot of effort into your ad, the perceived value will increase for the recipient. Because your beautiful animation impresses, the motivation to take a chance on you increases.

Please note: do not spend your entire budget on animations. We have seen email campaigns with beautiful animated GIFs convert very poorly because the other guidelines in this chapter were not applied. Complicated copy, an overly busy design, and a mediocre subject line will easily cancel out the potential benefit of an animated GIF.

HOW TO APPLY BEHAVIORAL PSYCHOLOGY
Search engine ads

For many brands and companies, advertising in search engines such as Google has become a core part of their online marketing campaigns. Let's examine how the principles in this book can help you to get more people to click on the ads at the top of the search results.

At first glance, search engine ads look a little bit like display ads. But if you look at them from a behavior design point of view, you suddenly see big differences. Just like ads on social media, banners are an example of interruption marketing: they 'disturb' people while they are doing something else. But with search engine ads, people come to you with a clear question. As a sender, you actually don't interrupt anyone.

Suppose David wants to buy a new laptop. His search query may look something like this:

    Q Best laptop

Or maybe he types a complete question, something we see more and more often:

    Q What is the best laptop today?

Next, several ads appear at the top of the search results. One of them is yours; the rest is from your competition. And your aim is to beat them. You do this by attracting attention and increasing motivation. We will now deal with both.

Top-down attention

With search engine ads, attracting attention works a little differently. If your user has a particular query in mind, the literal representation of that query will attract the most attention. We also call this 'top-down attention'. Let's take a look at the results of David's search:

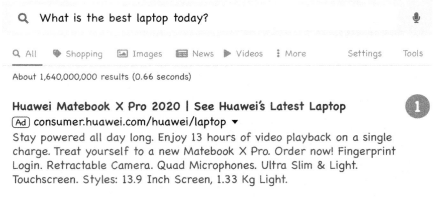

① This ad copy does not match the search terms. It's clear that the visitor is still orientating and wants to compare. Knowing this, The 'Buy it now' call to action is a pretty big commitment.

② This ad title perfectly matches the visitor's search terms, because it offers an independent comparison. 'Which.co.uk' is a well-known independent authority.

Of course, having your ad at the top is an advantage. There is a good chance that it will be read first, purely because of the number 1 position. However, ranking is not the only factor at play. If your ad literally contains the search query, it attracts more attention than ads that don't. In the example, the ads of Huawei and which.co.uk are more in line with David's demand. If you really want to get it spot on, you should actually use the question form. The following example literally contains David's question:

What is the best laptop? | Independent comparison | This is the top-10
[Ad] www.laptopmonster.com/ ▼
Best laptops and best value for money. Independent comparison.
Check them out now.

Our advice is simple: include in your ad what visitors are asking themselves, and if they literally recognize their question, it feels like a 'match made in heaven'. And that's what you are after.

It also helps if you can show a good sellers' rating, in the form of four or five stars.[43] The stars attract extra attention and give confidence, which can increase your click-through ratio (CTR) by up to 10 percent.

Motivation boosters

If your ad is a concrete feedback of the search intention of your target group, you can reinforce it with motivation boosters. Please note: you should not use the motivational strategies in this book as the *main message* of your ad. System 1 is most sensitive to an answer to the specific search question of your target group, as explained in the section above. So, start the ad with the search intention and, as a rule, place a motivation booster – not the other way around:

👍 **Do**

Start with the search intention, followed by the motivation booster. In this example, the booster is social proof.

A new laptop... | What to look for?
[Ad] www.laptopscompared.com/ ▼
45,499 professionals have already compared laptops.
Make your own comparison.

👎 **Don't**

Start with the motivation booster, followed by the search intention.

45,499 professionals compared here | Make your own comparison
[Ad] www.laptopscompared.com/ ▼
A new laptop: what to look for?

Below are three more concrete examples of the application of motivation boosters: scarcity, anticipatory enthusiasm, and reasons why in combination with loss aversion:

Motivation booster 1: scarcity

A new laptop... | What to look for?
[Ad] www.laptopscompared.com/ ▼
Don't wait too long, serious discounts in February only. Compare here.

Motivation booster 2: anticipatory enthusiasm

A new laptop... | What to look for?
[Ad] www.laptopscompared.com/ ▼
Open up the laptop that suits you perfectly. Make your own comparison.

Motivation booster 3: reasons why + loss aversion

A new laptop... | What to look for?
[Ad] www.laptopscompared.com/ ▼
Because good research before buying prevents bad buys.
Make your own comparison.

Jenga technique

Finally, a practical tip: use the Jenga technique. (See *The Jenga technique* chapter in Part 4). Search engines set requirements for the number of letters and words you can use in your ad. These restrictions change all the time, but at the time of writing this book, a headline can consist of thirty characters, including spaces. This is limiting, but with the Jenga technique you will almost always be able to shorten your message. First write down everything that comes to mind and then remove all unnecessary words. You do not have to aim for the maximum number; the shorter the text, the greater the chance that it will be read.

HOW TO APPLY BEHAVIORAL PSYCHOLOGY

Landing pages

Once you've tempted your visitors with an ad or email, they are directed to your landing page. This is where the persuasion process really begins. On your landing page, your visitors determine whether they will take a chance on you or go back to what they were doing.

The conversion rate of a landing page is on average around 4 percent, depending on the sector and industry. It's an interesting fact, but no more than that. The value of your 'performance' cannot be separated from the costs you have incurred to get your visitor to your landing page. For example, a conversion rate of 0.4 percent can be quite profitable, as long as the advertising costs are low enough. So don't be fixated on this type of benchmark.

Hopefully that 4 percent will make you aware that most visitors do not normally do what you want. Don't let that intimidate you.

There is no such thing as the perfect template
You can find all kinds of templates online for 'the ideal landing page'. From experience, we can tell you that such a template does not exist. Sometimes an extensive landing page with sub-pages works best; other times a short and concise page is more effective. Successful landing pages come in all shapes and sizes.

The ideal size and layout for you depends on the type of product you offer and the type of behavior you ask for.

One distinction here is the extent to which your customers can still reverse their decision.

With a paid online course, or other forms of paid online content, in most cases you cannot get your money back because you are given immediate access and benefits. In such cases, potential students will want to know all the ins and outs in advance. What will I learn? What does the course material look like? Who is the teacher? Who are the other students? What are the entry requirements? You have to answer all these questions on your landing page if you want to persuade someone to sign up.

However, if the commitment you require is less significant, for example when you ask your visitor to install a trial version of an app, then your page does not have to be that extensive, but should mainly tempt people to register for a month for free. For example, when making an appointment for a sales meeting, you need to provide much less information than when selling online content, because after showing the desired behavior, your visitor is still not bound to anything.

So, consider the balance between the commitment you ask someone to make in time and money, and adjust the 'comprehensiveness' of your landing page accordingly.

Provide a soft landing

Another aspect of a good landing page is the 'soft' landing. Let's compare it to a business meeting.

Suppose you have an appointment at someone's office in a large, new building. As soon as you have passed the reception, you walk through corridors with white walls, concrete floors and the occasional abstract work of art. Once arrived at your business contact's office, however, everything looks completely different: the burgundy floor is made of wood, the walls are covered with traditional English floral wallpaper and an antique chandelier dangles from the ceiling. That's when doubt strikes. Have you come to the right place? System 1 sounds the alarm. It sends out an automatic warning signal that says: pay attention now, because something fishy is going on here.

Something similar may happen online if the design of your landing page differs too much from that of your ad. If that transition does not feel logical, people will experience mild stress. The uncomfortable consequence of such a 'hard' landing is that your visitors – whom you took great pains to direct to your landing page – often go back to where they came from. That's what you want to avoid:

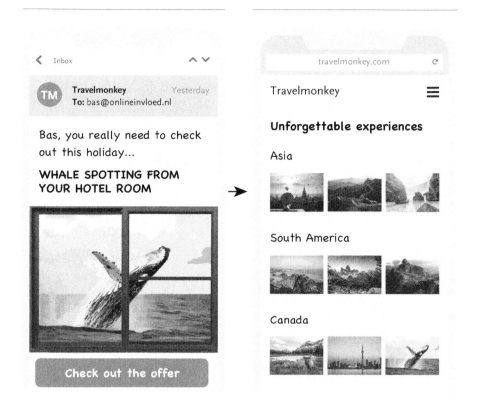

You avoid this by ensuring a soft landing: a logical transition from ad to landing page. Visually and textually align your landing page with your ad, for example, by using the same pictures, color palettes and fonts. But also, by using (almost) identical texts. After their click, your visitors need these kinds of recognizable elements to be able to trust that they have clicked correctly:

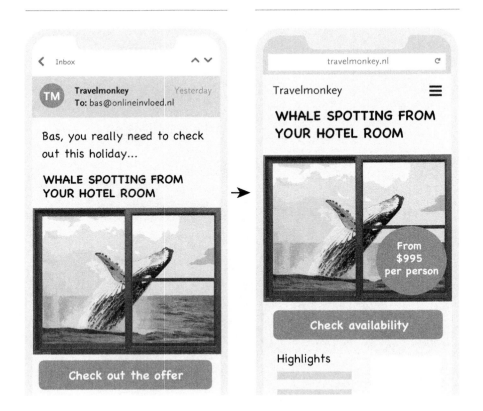

Also soften the cookie notification

If you've designed a nice soft landing, there's another danger. Cookie notifications are becoming more and more extensive due to privacy laws and, despite your design for a soft landing, still cause a stressful transition. Try to make sure the cookie notification doesn't take up too large a part of the page and adjust the design to match that of your campaign.

Consider your main visual

One defining part of your landing page is the first visual your visitors see. In professional terms, we also call it the 'main visual' or 'hero image'. It's great if your design contains multiple images or videos, but it's important to understand that the first image your visitors see is decisive in their choice of whether or not to stay on your landing page. The first impression is the most significant one.

New product: offer clarity

For example, if you have a new product that people are not really familiar with yet, use a main visual that helps your visitors to understand your product, which will increase their ability. So, when promoting a new app, show the frame of a mobile phone, containing an explanatory and distinctive screenshot of the app. Don't show a log-in screen, because every app has one.

Familiar product: motivate

If you have a product of which you can assume that visitors know what it is and how it works, consider using a main visual that motivates them. A good way to do that is to strike the right emotional chord with your visitors. For example, if you are selling a family outing, open with a picture of a happy and relaxed family. If you are selling a training course, show people who are getting their diploma, or people who are diligently using their acquired knowledge in a professional context.

Not sure which main visual to use? Always opt for something visual that increases your visitors' ability. Because if they don't understand what exactly you are offering, they won't become a customer anyway. Ignorance is bliss, but not when it comes to conversion.

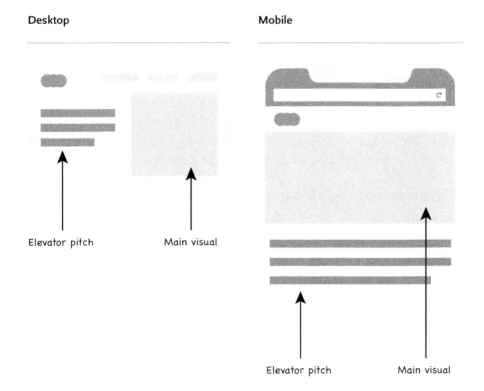

Give an elevator pitch

Suppose you are in an elevator with a wealthy investor. You have five seconds to pitch your business plan between the second and eleventh floors. You will give it your all, right? With a short, but convincing elevator pitch you might just convince him to give you his business card. The online world is not all that different: there, too, you have five seconds to make your impression and attract your visitors' attention.

Elevator Pitch

Keep it short

Your online elevator pitch has to be short, and preferably visible in a large font. This maximizes its chances of being read. Because we usually tend to scroll past lengthy texts in a small font. So, try tell your visitors something in two sentences that together take up no more than three lines.

Tell them what you have to offer

What you tell visitors in your elevator pitch should at the very least be about what they can do on that page. In other words: what do you have to offer? Because that's what it's all about. If you have any lines left, you can spend some words on a distinctive feature or a unique part.

Align your text and call to action

There is often a button directly under the elevator pitch: the call to action. The beauty of this button, and the text on it, is that it immediately makes clear to your visitors what they can do on your site. This means you don't have to tell them in your elevator pitch. In other words, try to align the design of the elevator pitch and the call to action. Take a look at the following examples:

👍 Clear

It is clear what you can and cannot do and what your advantage is.

Lend money to small entrepreneurs in emerging countries at an attractive interest rate of 3%. Choose a project that suits you.

👎 Not clear

Here, it is not clear whether you can lend or borrow and if it is a site where you are able to do something. It could just as well be a blog about entrepreneurs in emerging countries.

Loans for small entrepreneurs in emerging countries.

👍 👍 Even better

The 'Choose a project' button makes it clear that you can choose a project here. So, you don't need to mention this in your elevator pitch.

Lend money to small entrepreneurs in emerging countries at an attractive interest rate of 3%.

Choose a project

Clear
It is clear that this is about e-learning and that they execute projects.

 Not clear
This could mean anything

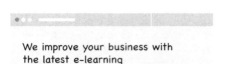

We improve your business with the latest e-learning technology.

Improving business performance through award-winning solutions.

Contrary to the texts we use in interruption marketing (see the *Online advertising* chapter), the text of an elevator pitch focuses on System 2. So, although you shouldn't design that pitch for a 7-year-old kid, you should still keep it simple. Otherwise there is a risk that your visitors will not understand the text within five seconds.

THE FIVE-SECOND TEST
An easy way to test if your elevator pitch complies with the five-second rule is to ask a random passer-by to look at your design for five seconds. This can be a simple sketch (wireframe), as long as the combination of main visual, text and call to action can be seen. If the passer-by understands what it is you offer after five seconds, your elevator pitch is short enough and still clear.

Features or benefits?

Here's a dilemma you might recognize as an online marketer: should you communicate the features or the benefits? There is no unambiguous answer to that question. It depends entirely on your product or service, and the extent to which your visitors are familiar with it. Take a look at these two elevator pitches:

Benefits	Features
X helps you wrangle people with different roles, responsibilities, and objectives toward a common goal: Finishing a project together.	Y is a platform for team communication: everything in one place, instantly searchable, available wherever you go.

The first pitch describes the advantage of product X. But what exactly is X? Is it a workshop? A tool? Or a person? This is not clear. This is why the second pitch seems much better. It makes it clear that this is a software application with at least two features: a search function and the fact that you can use the application on all your devices.

It depends

We didn't make these two pitches up. The first one was on Basecamp's website, the second one on Slack's. These two companies offer competitive tools for online collaboration, and thus pitch a similar product. Naming the benefits and the ultimate 'usefulness' of your product can be convincing if you are sure that visitors already know your product. Exactly like Basecamp did. But if your visitors have no idea yet what kind of product you are offering, naming those advantages and their usefulness will not be enough to convince them. For this reason, the then unknown company Slack probably decided to concretely state in its pitch that it offered a software tool. The ideal content of your pitch, therefore, depends on the extent to which visitors know your product.

Tell people why you are better

Sometimes the benefits of your product are so obvious that it doesn't need persuasion value. In that case, it is wiser to focus on distinctive product properties in your elevator pitch. Cars are a striking example of this. Naming the useful feature of a car has no impact, because it applies to all cars. But the fact that your car has a large fuel tank that will take you on a 600-mile journey without refueling, does make a difference. Therefore, when creating an elevator pitch, always make a well-considered choice between 'what', 'why' and 'why am I better than the other'.

Use the power of three

'Three' has a magical effect in the world of persuasion. A study by behavioral scientists Kurt Karlson and Suzanne Shu showed that people find three benefits more convincing than two, four, five or six benefits.[44] Why, you ask? Two benefits are less impressive, and four or more benefits can come across as boastful. Moreover, visitors will appreciate it if you have already thought about the three most important benefits rather than giving them a huge list:

👍 Do	👎 Don't
Three benefits	Two or four benefits
✔ Whiter teeth	✔ Whiter teeth
✔ Healthy gums	✔ Healthy gums
✔ Fresh breath	✔ Reduced risk of caries
	✔ Fresh breath

Please note: this is mainly a summary of your benefits. It is best to display such a list at the top of your landing page, for example, immediately below your elevator pitch. If you are struggling to determine the most important benefits, you can ask your customers with an online poll or a questionnaire.

All other benefits can be mentioned in other places on your landing page, for example, in the running text or in the form of a testimonial.

Earn trust

Once your visitors have an initial idea of what you have to offer, it's time for the next step: earning trust. If you do not (yet) have a reputable name, your visitors will automatically look for evidence to decide whether you can be trusted. Therefore, use elements in the upper regions of your landing page that inspire this confidence. In an online environment, social proof and authority are ideally suited for this.

Social proof: reviews

Experience shows that it is becoming increasingly difficult to persuade online customers without reviews by other customers. Therefore, put a summary of their reviews at the top of your page, preferably with a score of at least eight out of ten stars, or at least four out of five stars. Also mention the total number of reviews and offer your visitors the option to browse all reviews. In this way, you can prevent them from thinking you've made the selection.

In addition to reviews, there are other ways to make visitors feel that they are not alone. You can use these if you have not collected any reviews or not enough reviews yet. For instance:

- Purchased 20 times today
- 1856 students obtained their diploma with us.
- 20 interested people are looking at this offer.
- This week, 239 professionals registered for a demo.

If you need more inspiration, please refer to the chapter on *Social Proof* in Part 3.

Authority: logos and quality labels

To gain visitors' trust, you can display logos and labels of trusted parties at the top of your landing page. This helps especially if your product is not yet well known. A few examples:

- Tested as best by the Consumer Association
- Member of the American E-learning Association
- BBB or NCVO quality label for charities
- Logos of newspapers that have written about you
- As seen on television (if you have been featured in a program or are running an advertising campaign on TV)
- Certifications you hold
- Awards and award nominations

In addition to these options, you can also highlight your own authority a little more. For example, by showing visitors your beautiful office or your team of experienced and well-trained professionals. You could also list the charities you support.

If you need more inspiration, please refer to the chapter on *Authority* in Part 3.

> Do not make authority logos, labels and content clickable. Otherwise, your visitors may leave the landing page for a reason other than the desired behavior.

Beautiful design = authority

Good news for all you stylish designers out there. An aesthetic, balanced and professional design increases your authority and gives visitors more confidence. That will also increase your conversion. In a survey by BJ Fogg, almost half of the respondents indicated that a beautiful design contributes to the trustworthiness of a website.[45]

But don't count your chickens before they are hatched. Buttons should not only be a feast for the eyes but also particularly clear. (See the *Affordance* chapter in Part 2.) And beautiful images should, above all, have a persuasive effect by fueling anticipation and their ability to explain your product. (See the *Anticipatory enthusiasm* chapter in Part 3.)

Persuade visually

Earlier, we talked about the main visual on your page. But visual communication is also essential for the rest of your landing page. As an online behavior designer, you will hopefully have access to a substantial library of pictures and videos. Or you may have a budget for a photo shoot or – as a last resort only – high-quality stock photos. When choosing your images, you should consider three persuasion strategies: generate anticipatory enthusiasm, visualize the underlying need, and offer an explanation.

Generate anticipatory enthusiasm

The first persuasion strategy for your photos and videos: show your visitors the reward they can expect after doing the desired behavior. This generates 'anticipatory enthusiasm'. (See the chapter of the same name in Part 3). You could, for example, show the physical product that they will receive in the future, but also the moment of unpacking, the use of the product, and perhaps even the end result. Rewards that are instantaneous or in the very near future have the strongest effect on our unconscious brain, but you can also create this enthusiastic effect with rewards that are a little further in the future. A few examples:

What are you selling?	Immediate reward: more instantaneous	Postponed reward: more value
Design software	A number of screenshots or a video of the software screens	The end result: a successful design and a satisfied customer
An online course	A sneak preview of the teaching materials that will be accessible	Students proudly holding up their diploma
Consultancy	The consultancy in practice, for example, a consultant who visits the client and creates a problem-solving design	More profit and better collaboration, for example, with an ascending graph and a team of people working in harmony

What are you selling?	Immediate reward: more instantaneous	Postponed reward: more value
A flying holiday	A preview of the ticket that will be emailed later	The comfortable flight itself, or a nice destination, a relaxed feeling when you return home or a photo album with special memories

Visualize the underlying basic need

The second persuasion strategy for your photos and videos: visualize your visitors' underlying needs. You can do his by showing the positive emotional impact of your product. (See also the chapter *Appealing to basic needs* in Part 3.) A few examples:

What are you selling?	Underlying need	Visual
Winter coats	Comfort, not being cold	Someone who braves the cold with a smile, wearing the winter coat in a winter landscape
Expensive winter coats	Being accepted and admired	Someone wearing the winter coat surrounded by a group of friends
Insurance	Safety, no risk	A family that clearly doesn't have a care in the world

Explain

The third persuasion strategy for your photos and videos: use illustrations and infographics that explain how your product or service works. A picture often says more than a thousand words, this also applies in online environments. And the better your visitors understand how it works, the more likely they are to say yes:

What are you selling?	What should you explain?	Visual support
A dating app	How the app works	Show *screenshots* that explain how the main features work
A modem	How to install the modem	Design a series of *illustrations* showing how to install a modem.

What are you selling?	What should you explain?	Visual support
A property valuation	How the procedure works	Visualize the steps using *photography*: customer calls for an appointment, the surveyor drops by, and the same customer receives their valuation report.

The right mix
So, use a mix of different types of images to persuade visually – one to hit the right emotional chord, the other to explain how your product works. You don't have to worry about having enough room for all those images, because a landing page can be quite long. What's more, you can also take small trips from your landing page. We will elaborate on this later on in this chapter.

Use video, but use it wisely

With a video, you can show your product and how it works in an attractive way. This can greatly benefit your conversion, provided your video meets several requirements. If it doesn't, videos are often counterproductive. There are four things to keep in mind: be predictable, don't beat about the bush, be careful with background videos and use a play button.

Be predictable
For starters, it should be completely clear to your visitors beforehand what the video is about. The online video offering is huge and people know that watching videos takes time. That's why they are often a little hesitant; they don't want to start a video only to find out after ten seconds that it doesn't match their expectations. By making it clear on the home screen what the video is about, you take that feeling away. A few examples of how you can achieve this:

- Take a look at an impression of our workshop.
- Edward talks about the five unique properties of our powder coating.
- How to assemble this piece of furniture.

Don't beat about the bush
In addition, it is smart to start stating your message immediately. Many online videos start with a flashy introduction of five to ten seconds, often with suspenseful music and an animated logo. That may work on television, if people have consciously sat down to watch. Online, however, it's a waste of time. Your visitors should have already spotted your logo in the top left corner. What's

more, when online, they prefer to get to the point immediately. So, get down to business straight away.

Watch out with background videos
Be careful with background videos. This type of video can generate a high-end feeling to your page, but it will only work if it is subtle and does not distract from the text on the landing page itself. A busy video often makes it unnecessarily difficult for visitors to concentrate. Which, in turn, reduces the chance of conversion.

Use a play button
Finally, visitors should never have to think about how to start the video. A play button is, therefore, indispensable to create sufficient affordance.

A back button is better than navigation
Sometimes you have so much to say about your product or service that your landing page will be very long if you were to list everything. In such cases, you may be inclined to design a campaign website with several pages, with a main navigation and possibly a sub-navigation. The disadvantage is that this approach greatly increases the complexity of the interaction:

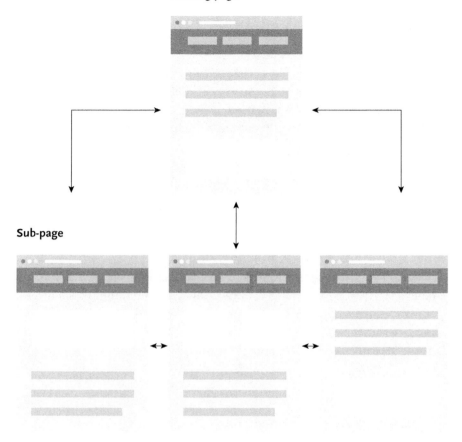

Moreover, displaying a menu invites visitors to play around with it. In terms of the Fogg Behavior Model: showing a menu is a strong prompt to navigate. And that's usually not the desired behavior.

It's preferable if your visitors take in the persuasive content in the order that you have so carefully put together, in order to always take the next step towards final conversion. So, if you want to keep control and reduce complexity, it is better to use detail pages than build a website structure. Detail pages offer only one interaction: going back to the landing page via a close button or a back button. In this way, your visitors make small side trips, but they always come back to your landing page:

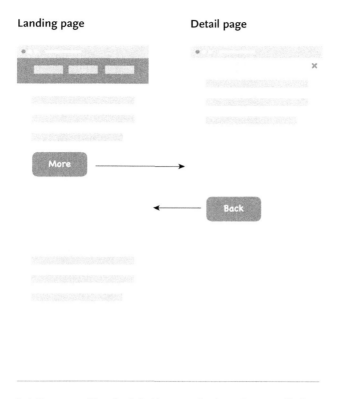

Detail pages with a back button are simple and ensure that you keep control over your visitors' route.

Zooming in and out on a detail page requires less mental effort from your visitors than operating a navigation and sub-navigation. In addition, a detail page gives you more control over your visitors' routes, allowing for better control of the desired behavior.

> The back button on your detail page is the prompt to the behavior you want to see. So, give that button a 'sticky' design: it should always be visible and tempt visitors to return to your landing page.

Provide clear structure

Some landing pages need many different information blocks to inform and persuade visitors. Rhythm and clear headings help you to hold your visitors' attention.

Rhythm
Keep the information blocks short and make the heads scannable. This infuses your page with rhythm. (See the concrete tips in the *Page Structure* chapter in Part 4.)

Headings
Think of the headings on your landing page as 'prompts to continue reading' that encourage your visitors to keep scrolling. They should attract attention, in other words. You can achieve this by making them large enough or providing them with a light animation, which starts as soon as you can reasonably expect your visitor to have read or scanned the previous block.

The use of the question form makes scanning easy. The content of the content block answers the question asked in the heading. For example:

- How does the installation work?
- What are the entry requirements?
- How soon will I get access?

If you choose the question form, make sure you do so consistently. This will improve your visitor's ability to efficiently take in the information. If you want to make your headings more persuasive, you can use the Curiosity strategy or the Exceptional-benefit strategy. (See the chapters of the same name in Part 2.)

Exceptional benefit:
- No more fogged-up glasses
- Free repair kit when ordering before January 1st

Curiosity:
- This is what our students say
- Three reasons not to do it

Communicate scarcity

By communicating scarcity, you give your visitors a reason to act immediately instead of later. If scarcity is the 'hook' of your campaign, we advise you to communicate it at the top of your landing page. A few examples:

- Only 72 early-bird tickets left
- This promotion ends in 2 days
- There are still 47 seats available

One condition is that your visitors fully understand your product or service and are enthusiastic about it. Otherwise, the quick deployment of the Scarcity principle can cause irritation and frustration. So, if your product is still new or not yet completely clear, start by creating trust followed by a desire for your product or service; then communicate the scarcity – subtly and factually:

Scarcity

[Check availability]

Neutral, no scarcity

[View products]

Calls to action

The first behavior that you need once your visitors have landed, is that they read your text and view your carefully selected videos and images. You can then design a call to action that acts as a prompt for the next micro behavior. Consider entering personal data, configuring the product or choosing from different packages, for example.

Not everyone feels the need to dig through all the text and images to be persuaded. That's why it's smart to not only place a call to action at the bottom of your page, but in various places. You could also make the call to action 'sticky', so that the page scrolls on underneath the button. Doing so risks creating a kind of adaptation behavior, however, comparable to banner blindness. By subtly moving the button from time to time, you let your visitor know what you want them to do.

Above the fold?

A common rule in the world of conversion is that the call to action must be within the visible part of the web page: 'within the viewport' or 'above the fold'. Fortunately, A/B tests demonstrate that this is not necessary at all. In fact, conversion is sometimes even higher if you don't immediately ask visitors to click. And if you do want to do this, it is often difficult to cram your elevator pitch, the benefits of your product or service, and your main visual onto a small (mobile) screen. Moreover, that kind of cramming doesn't do anything for the look and simplicity of your design.

At the same time, you should not put your call to action too low on your landing page. This button has both a functional and informative value: your call-to-action text makes it clear what your visitors can do on the page:

Button	Informative value
Configure	Immediately makes it clear that people can configure and customize your product.
To checkout	Immediately explains that people can order this product online; this is not always obvious.

Use baby steps

If you are unsure whether to use a hard or soft call to action, soft ones will generally work better. They contain a small step rather than a big commitment. Compare the following button texts:

Hard call to action	Soft call to action
Invest	Decide how much you want to invest
Subscribe now	Configure your subscription
Order	To checkout

So, when do hard calls to action work better? For example, if you have a temporary promotion with a low price. In this case, texts such as 'Order now' and 'Register now' sometimes work better, because they emphasize the sense of scarcity.

If your landing page is attracting plenty of visitor traffic, we recommend experimenting with your calls to action. You will soon find out which one works best for you.

Add benefits

You can make your call to action more attractive by incorporating a benefit. However, only do this if you can keep it simple:

👍 **Sufficiently simple**

A call to action with a benefit only works if it is phrased sufficiently simply

[Try for free]

[Order with a discount]

[Donate: save a life]

👎 **Too complicated**

Button text too long

[Order and benefit from this temporary promotion today only]

A long button text as shown in the latter example is not only difficult to read, but your button will also have to be excessively wide. As a result, the button no longer feels like a button, which reduces affordance. (See the *Affordance* chapter in Part 2.)

HOW TO APPLY BEHAVIORAL PSYCHOLOGY

Product detail pages

If you offer more than one product in your online environment, make a separate product detail page for each product. Doing so will enable you to provide all the information needed to convince your visitors to order the product. This is why product detail pages play a crucial role in online influence.

In many ways, product detail pages are similar to landing pages. That is why many of the principles and applications from the previous chapter can also be used for product detail pages. But some practical tips and applications are specific to these pages. We will list them in this chapter, with a focus on physical products that you can order online, although most of these principles can also be used for digital products.

Product detail page as 'the center of the universe'

Ordering a product online sometimes demands a lot from your customers, mainly because they do not have the product physically in their hands and do not have direct contact with a seller or adviser. So, in most cases, your visitors are entirely dependent on the information you provide on your product detail page.

Research shows that high-conversion product detail pages tend to answer any questions that visitors may have. You can find out which questions people ask by carefully examining the questions that (potential) customers ask via customer service, or by conducting research. (See the *Conversion Research* chapter further on in this Part.)

These questions are often not about the product itself, but about the ordering process:

- How will I get the product?
- What are the delivery options?
- Are there any additional costs?
- Will the package be delivered to the neighbors if I am not at home?
- Does the delivery person assemble the product, or do I have to do it myself?

Many online providers make the mistake of only providing the delivery information on a general page. But chances are that your visitors will end up directly on the product detail page via a search engine, comparison site, or ad. In addition, online shoppers often have browser windows from multiple webshops open. As soon as they get to the point where they want to know how and when a product is delivered, that information must be immediately available. If that is not the case, they will have to start looking for that information. As a result, a lot of time is lost and you – unnecessarily – demand a lot of their mental effort. As a result, their ability decreases, and with that, the chance of conversion.

Make sure that the product detail pages offer all the relevant information about a product. Doing so may feel repetitive, but having all the information in one place is nice and clear for your visitors, especially if they are comparing your offer with that of other providers.

That is why you should think of the product detail page as 'the center of the universe.' In any event, it should always contain the following information:

- product photos
- product information
- reviews
- information about the buying process
- information about the final price
- information about you, the provider

We will now examine all these parts in more detail.

Product photos

Images of your product are absolutely vital. They ensure that your visitors can vividly imagine possessing and using your product, which creates anticipatory enthusiasm. (See the chapter of the same name in Part 3.)

Many experiments show that the larger and more realistic the picture, the greater the chance of conversion. Websites with only minuscule product images sell significantly fewer products. In addition, it is preferable to use multiple pictures. So, try to photograph your products from all possible angles, and use close-ups to show important details to help your visitors imagine the product.

Successful webshops often present the various product pictures as a row of thumbnails (small images) that visitors can easily click on. This is smart because enlarging product pictures and zooming in on details contribute to the sense that visitors are holding the product in their hands. And if consumers have physical contact with a product, according to consumer researchers Joann Peck and Suzanne Shu, this leads to a higher valuation of that product and higher estimation of its value.[46]

To fully anticipate the use of a product, you can show pictures of people unpacking or using it. Please note that your visitors should be able to identify with the people in your images, otherwise it may backfire. For example, don't use pictures of very young people if you're targeting over-50s.

Another tip: take pictures from eye level. The same applies to videos. This point of view helps your visitors to realistically imagine possessing and using your product. The more you help your visitors with that, the more enthusiasm you will generate.

Cheerleader effect

Interesting fact: when we judge someone who is in a group photo surrounded by attractive people, we find that person 'more beautiful' than when he or she is alone in the photo. We unconsciously project the beautiful qualities of a group of people onto all individuals in that group. In psychology, this is also called the 'cheerleader effect'.[47]

As a behavior designer, you can use this effect to increase the perceived value of your products. (See also the chapter with the same name in Part 3.) You can add a product to a series of products that you know your visitors find attractive, for example. We like a standard frying pan better when it is part of a complete pan set with state-of-the-art pans. And a charging cable, for example, looks much better next to a shiny iPhone than it does on its own:

👍 **Cheerleader effect**
The charging cable becomes more valuable when placed next to the expensive telephone.

👎 **On its own**
Feels less valuable.

Product information

The more questions you answer about your product, the fewer questions your visitors will have to ask. When you provide product information, you should certainly pay attention to the following aspects:

- **What does the product do for the customer?**
  This sports drink provides energy during exercise and restores the muscles afterward.

- **What makes the product work?**
  This cream contains argireline. This substance relaxes your facial muscles, so you are less likely to get wrinkles.

- **What makes the product unique?**
  This bike is the cheapest city bike in our range.

What often also works well is a list of the most important properties of your product. In practice, such a bullet point list mainly helps on product detail pages of useful and technical products, such as gadgets and nutritional supplements. With luxury products and designer items, a list or table of properties is more likely to detract from the 'luxurious' feeling. An attractively written text is often a better option in that case.

Finally, it is a good idea to provide a summary of the most important information. You can hide less important information (such as detailed specifications) behind a click to keep your product details page clear and easy to scan. (See also the *Landing Pages* chapter in this part of the book.)

Reviews

These days, it is difficult to sell products online without credible reviews. In the *Social Proof* chapter, we provided a list of tips to help you present reviews in the best possible way. (See Part 3.)

People often ask us how many reviews it takes to have social proof work for you. As far as we are concerned, there is no 'standard lower limit'; the minimum number of reviews required depends on your product. For more expensive purchases, for example, we tend to look for a little more confirmation. As a rule of thumb, the more reviews, the better, and the more peer reviews, the better.

If you have fewer than ten reviews about a product, general reviews about your webshop offer a possible solution to provide sufficient social proof.

Information about the buying process

For your conversion, delivery information is at least as important as the product information itself. Therefore, communicate information about the buying process before people order.

If you are ordering a gift for your partner, for example, you want to make sure you will get it on time, and that you will be there to take the package at a time when your partner is not at home. In practice, we have observed that many product detail pages do not facilitate this. These are missed opportunities.

In addition, keep the payment method, the time and method of delivery in mind when you design or analyze your product detail page. We will walk you through them.

Payment method
Tell users early on in the process how they will be able to pay (and not just at checkout). For example, answer the following questions:

- What are the payment methods?
- Is there a charge if I pay with my credit card?
- Can I pay in installments?
- Can I pay on delivery?

Time
Provide clarity and certainty about time aspects. Consider these questions:

- When will I receive the product?
- When will I receive an invoice?
- When do I get access? (In the case of a digital product.)
- Until when can I cancel my order?
- What is the payment term?

Delivery method
Explain how the product delivery works. For example, based on these questions:

- Will the parcel fit through the mailbox?
- Will the parcel fit through the door?
- Do I have to stay at home to receive the parcel?
- What happens to my parcel if I am not at home?
- Will my parcel be delivered on the third floor?

If you do not answer the questions within these themes, this can already lead to dropout behavior. The longer it takes to find the answer, the higher the chance that your visitor will change their mind. So, place this type of information in a findable place and use clear headings that are written from the customers' point of view. Here are three examples:

From the organization's point of view (not clear)	From the customer's point of view (clear)
Delivery terms and conditions	When will I receive the product?
Ordering procedure	How does ordering work?
Delivery information	Will the parcel fit through the mailbox?

Information about the final price

Be clear about the price of a product or service. When we look at the paths that visitors take, we sometimes see that they only navigate to the end of the checkout to see what the final amount of their order will be.

Why is that? Perhaps because many sites add extra costs at a later stage in the customer journey. We don't think that's wise. By being entirely transparent from the start, you can save your visitors a lot of time. Besides, they will appreciate your openness, which will increase their ability as well as their motivation. That is why you should always state the total price on your product detail page, including all delivery costs, administration costs, booking fees, and other costs.

Free delivery

Nobody likes to pay for delivery. In fact, paying more for a product feels less bad than paying an additional amount for delivery. This is why – where possible – it is always better to offer free delivery. You can incorporate the delivery costs you incur into the price of your product:

👍 Do	👎 Don't	
45.-	Price:	40.-
Free delivery	Delivery fee:	5.-
	Total:	**45.-**

Please note: this advice works particularly well with unique products. If visitors can also buy the same product in another webshop, it may seem as if you are charging more. To avoid this, it would be smarter for retailers to state the delivery costs separately.

Price perception

Retailers try their best, both offline and online, to make prices feel as low as possible. It is useful to know that the emotion we feel when we see a price (cheap or expensive) is partly determined by the way the price is presented.[48] As an online behavior designer, keep in mind the following two rules of thumb for price perception:

- Spend as few pixels as possible on what something is going to cost.
- Visually emphasize what the visitor is going to receive.

To clarify, we'll give you some examples.

Omit currency characters

You may have noticed that most major webshops do not include currency signs on their product detail pages. They have found that omitting them leads to an increase in conversion. Please make sure that it is clear to visitors that the number shown is the price:

👍 Do   👎 Don't
_____   _____
45.-   **$ 45.-**

Disclaimer: if your webshop supports multiple currencies, it is preferable to show the currency sign, to avoid confusion.

Do not use a large font
Do not use a giant font for your prices. The smaller the font, the less expensive a product feels unconsciously. One exception to that rule would be an amazing offer, in which case it's an excellent idea to shout the price from the rooftops.

Do not use decimal places
The more digits, the more expensive something feels. So if the decimal places don't matter, don't show them:

👍 Do   👎 Don't
_____   _____
45.-   **45.00**
45

Use non-rounded figures for useful products
Research shows that non-rounded figures (like 4.59) feel fairer than rounded ones (like 4.50). Please note that this effect only occurs with so-called utility products that are generally considered useful, such as batteries and equipment.

Do use rounded figures for luxury products
If you offer luxury products, digits after the decimal point actually feel 'rational'. And that does not fit very well with this product category. That is why it's better to use rounded figures (such as 120) for luxurious products.

From-for construction
Earlier in this book, we discussed anchoring: how people experience an amount of money as less if they have seen a higher amount shortly before. The highest price in a classic from-for construction can be such an anchor:

👍 Do	👎 Don't
400.- 349.-	Now 349.-

An additional advantage of this construction is that the perceived value of the product increases. After all, system 1 thinks: the more expensive, the better. (See the *Perceived Value* chapter in part 3.)

Repeat the discount
It is also a good idea to repeat a discount. As a result, you will automatically spend more pixels on what your visitors receive than on what something will cost them:

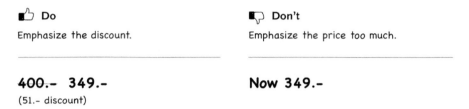

👍 Do	👎 Don't
Emphasize the discount.	Emphasize the price too much.
400.- 349.- (51.- discount)	Now 349.-

Making an amount feel as high as possible
Finally, you may want to make an amount appear higher, for example, when you mention a discount or when you want to communicate the value of free incentives. In that case, the reverse of all the above rules applies:

👍 Do	👎 Don't
A free suitcase worth **$ 900.- DOLLARS**	A free suitcase worth 900.-

Information about you as a provider

People who shop online often end up on your product detail page via a search engine, comparison site, or ad. This means that their journey usually doesn't take them via your homepage. If your webshop is not very well known, there is a good chance that your visitors will at some point wonder: who are these guys anyway? If that happens, you don't want them to go to your homepage, away from your persuasive product page.

That is why you should tell people something about yourself on your product detail page. It doesn't have to be an elaborate story; a summary is enough. It's about being able to answer your visitors' most important questions. For instance:

Part	Example	Persuasion
What does your company do?	We supply ink cartridges for all types of printers.	You offer clarity and confirmation that you are the right company.
What is your proposition?	Our mission is to serve our customers as quickly as possible so that they can continue to do their work.	You come across as more sympathetic when you show the value you offer your customers.
Who are your customers?	We deliver to companies and individuals all over the us.	This is a form of social proof (and, if your customers are well known, also a form of authority).
How long have you been around?	Since 1971 ...	The longer you have been around, the more authority.
Where are you based?	We supply from our own warehouses in Assen and Beverwijk.	Sharing physical locations instills confidence.

Even if you have an 'About Us' page, you should still provide information about yourself that plays a role in the persuasion process on your product detail pages.

Now that it is clear what information should not be missing from the product detail page, it is time to look at other aspects that make your product page more persuasive. We will successively deal with the layout, the use of live chat or a chatbot, the Scarcity principle, and the call to action.

The layout
The layout of your product detail page should make it easy for your visitors to find the information. Recognizability and rhythm are important in this.

Recognizability
Make your design similar to the layout of major webshops such as Amazon or Walmart. People often shop here and are used to how these websites work. If you deviate from this, you may make things unnecessarily complicated. You

will generally find the picture on the top left with the price, the delivery conditions, and the order button next to it. Also, take a look at how they display their reviews.

Rhythm
Introduce a rhythm to your landing pages and product detail pages. For example, put all the product information in a clear overview and make the headers of the various blocks easy to scan.

If you notice that the information blocks are getting too long, hide any detailed information behind a click. In other words, attach a details page to your details page, just like you do on your landing page.

Live chat or chatbot
This book is about automated persuasion without human intervention. Nevertheless, we would like to take a look at live chat and chatbots. One user-friendly way to answer visitor questions is an expert who answers via chat, which is why webshops with a live chat option often have a higher conversion rate. There are two conditions for success, however:

- **You need to be able to respond quickly.**
  People shop mostly outside of office hours, so you should also be available in the evenings and on weekends.

- **Employees should really be able to answer the questions.**
  In other words, they have to understand the product as well as the buying process.

If a live employee is not a profitable option, you could consider using a chatbot. Thanks to increasingly smart machine learning software, you can train it to answer the most frequently asked questions. If the chatbot fails, you can pass the question on to a human colleague.

Scarcity
Communicating scarcity lends itself very well to product detail pages. As you have read in the *Scarcity* chapter (in Part 3), there are two forms that you can use separately or simultaneously: scarcity in stock and scarcity in time.

Scarcity in stock
If your offer is limited in stock, it's a good idea to mention that:

> Only 5 left in stock

How small the stock needs to be to experience a sense of urgency depends entirely on the product. For a dining room table, 'Only 10 left in stock' doesn't feel all that scarce. With headphones that are on sale, however, the same announcement will make you feel that you have to act quickly.

In other words, scarcity in stock has a lot to do with the expectations visitors have about how quickly the stock is shrinking. To help visitors even better, you can make these expectations explicit:

> Expected to sell out within a few days

Did you know that merely seeing the word 'stock' affects System 1? That is why it is a good idea to mention that a product is 'in stock' even when there is sufficient stock. This communicates implicitly that the stock is finite and that products may sell out without warning, and creates a sense of urgency with your visitors.

Scarcity of time
If you have come up with a temporary promotion, do communicate it on your product details page, even if it applies to all your products. An example:

> Order today to receive a $5 voucher.

In addition, you can say something about the limited time visitors have to make sure they receive their order the next day to motivate people even more. For example, like this:

> Ordered before 23.59, delivered tomorrow!

Near the call to action
Because your product detail page usually contains a lot of information, we advise you to communicate scarcity in the vicinity of the call to action. Scarcity can then just give the necessary nudge to decide to buy.

The call to action

What applies to the call to action on your landing pages is also relevant for your product detail pages. However, three guidelines are particularly important here, which is why we will take you through them below: the soft call to action, Hobson + 1, and using shortcuts.

Soft call to action

You read earlier that asking for a small commitment is often more sensible than asking for a big commitment. (See the *Baby Steps* chapter in Part 3.) The same applies to your calls to action. That's why it's best to formulate them 'softly.' Here are three examples of soft alternatives to 'order':

- *In cart*
- *Add to cart*
- *Go to checkout*

If you have a good offer for a very scarce product (in time or stock), it is better to use a hard call to action, to emphasize the urgency. Three examples:

- *Order now*
- *Download now*
- *Register now*

Hobson + 1

Your visitors may still have doubts. If this happens, you don't want them to drop out completely and walk away, which is why you should also offer an alternative in addition to the primary call to action ('In cart') that attracts less visual attention. Three good alternatives:

- *Add to favorites*
- *Add to wish list*
- *Share with a friend*

Shortcuts

Using a shopping cart in your webshop has become the norm, but it is an extra step compared to direct ordering. For visitors who want to order an article quickly, it is nice if there is a direct route: a shortcut, which facilitates the buying behavior of these visitors. Three examples:

- *Take me to checkout*
- *Pay for this product now*
- *Order with one click*

HOW TO APPLY BEHAVIORAL PSYCHOLOGY
The checkout

And now for the last and perhaps most difficult part of the customer journey: the checkout. By checkout, we mean the screens your visitors have to go through after they have decided they want to buy your product or service. In other words: the place where they finally decide to do business with you.

Checkouts can be found in almost all online environments. During checkout in a webshop, you ask visitors for their address details, payment details, and a delivery method. For a newsletter checkout, you want visitors to leave their name, email address, and interests, or tick the box for an agreement. For the checkout of a lead generation promotion, the main thing is that your visitors fill in their contact details.

You may be wondering what these types of checkout have to do with online persuasion. If the actual persuasion has already taken place, it's just a matter of filling it in, right? Unfortunately, it's not that simple. Research into visitor flows shows that a staggering number of people drop out during checkout. In general, this is even more than 70 percent, as demonstrated in 41 studies between 2012 and 2019.[49]

Drop out explanation
This high percentage can be explained to a large extent with the Fogg Behavior Model: checking out takes effort and is usually a tedious job. If your visitors are not highly motivated at that time, there is a good chance that their interest will fade if things get too difficult. In addition, many visitors will be at work or the center of a busy household while ordering. As a result, they may be short on time or distracted by other things, and leave the checkout prematurely.

Another reason why visitors drop out is that they are far from convinced of their purchase when they are going through the checkout. This group only ends up on these screens to see if there are any snags, such as hidden costs or a very long delivery time.

Two assignments

As behavior designers, we consequently have two tasks when designing a checkout:

- make the checkout easy and efficient;
- continue to motivate visitors.

In this chapter, we will explain how to do that.

Let them complete as few details as possible

The Fogg Behavior Model predicts: the easier the checkout, the higher the conversion. In other words: minimize the amount of data you request from visitors. In the world of offline sales, there is a similar law: as soon as someone shows a willingness to buy, you have to close the deal as soon as possible.

So, ask yourself what data you really need. Birth dates, passport numbers, and telephone numbers, for example, are real conversion killers. So, don't ask for these if you don't need them (yet) to close the deal:

👎 **Don't**

Ask for details beforehand which you can just as easily ask for later on.

Enter your details

Your full name

Your email address

Your address

Your date of birth

Your passport number

Payment details

[Order and pay]

→

Thank you for your order

Offering additional products (upselling) is another cause of visitors dropping out. Everything you offer has to be assessed and can make your almost-customer doubt. So, save any upselling for later, preferably until after confirmation:

Do
Seal the deal as quickly as possible by asking for as few data as possible. Decide what data you can also ask for later on. Also check what data you can and cannot ask for later on, legally.

Smart webshops are designed in such a way that visitors can order additional products with one click after they have paid. And filling in an interest profile or passport number can also be done after giving permission for a newsletter or booking tickets.

Start by asking for information that is less personal

In the *Baby Steps* chapter (Part 3) we explained that it is better to start with small commitments rather than big ones. Small commitments include information that is not personal and that your visitors shouldn't have to think long about, like delivery preferences. Always save more significant commitments such as address information for last:

👍 **Do**
Ask for non-personal details first.

👎 **Don't**
Start with personal details.

How do you want to receive the book?

○
○

Enter your details

Your email address

Your full name

Your address

Enter your details

Your email address

Your full name

Your address

How do you want to receive the book?

○
○

If you end up asking your visitors for their address details, ask for the less personal details first. People leave their email address more easily than their phone number or home address. Especially in the latter case, they feel like they are revealing personal information. Entering a zipcode feels a lot safer, on the other hand:

👍 **Do**
Ask for non-personal details first.

👎 **Don't**
Start with the most personal details.

Divide forms into steps

Long forms can scare your visitors away. That's why you can often increase conversion by dividing a form into steps. Make sure that the first step feels simple, and limit the number of steps: preferably three to five. After all, a ten-step form is also intimidating:

👍 **Do**
Divide a long form into multiple steps. Show the steps in a progress bar.

👎 **Don't**
A very long form.

Configure

Address

Payment details

[To payment details]

Progress indicator
Many visitors like to have an idea of where they are in the process. A visual progress indicator (also called progress bar) increases the user-friendliness and, consequently, often the conversion too.

Don't start from zero
Don't let your visitors start from zero. They will be more motivated when they feel they're already halfway there. Therefore, always start with step 2, or at 50 percent. In psychology, the additional motivation they get through this 'gift' is called the 'endowed-progress effect'. (See box.)

In this progress bar, Zalando shows visitors immediately after logging in that they are already on their way:

Choose a subtle design

Your visitor's attention should always go to the prompt that asks for the desired behavior. This is usually the input field. The progress bar is a supporting element. So, keep it subtle and don't turn it into a complicated work of art. A simple line suffices on mobile screens:

👍 **Do**
A subtle progress bar, so that the form gets the attention.

👎 **Don't**
A complicated progress bar that diverts attention away from the form.

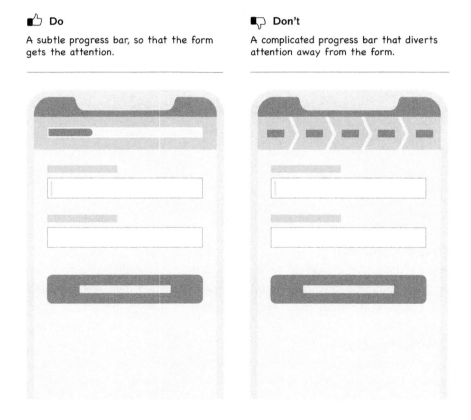

Sub-steps

If your forms have three to five steps, but they are still too long, you can opt for dividing one step into sub-steps. There is no need to name them in the progress bar. In the wireframe below, the second step consists of two sub-steps that are not named in the progress bar:

 Do

Use sub steps, to make sure that the progress bar does not become too long or complicated.

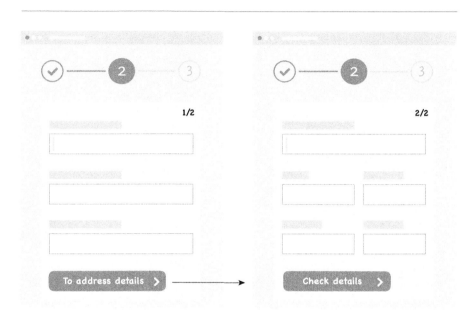

GIFTED PROGRESS: THE ENDOWED PROGRESS EFFECT

Marketing researchers Joseph Nunes and Xavier Drèze researched the effects of gifting your visitors some progress, for example, by letting them start at step 2.[50] They did this with an experiment at a gas station. Customers were given a stamp on a savings card after refueling; a full savings card with eight stamps entitled them to a free car wash.

The researchers designed two different savings cards: one with eight empty squares and one with ten squares, two of which were pre-stamped. The result? The savings card with the free stamps was redeemed by 34 percent of customers, the initially blank card only by 19 percent. In short: we feel more motivated when we feel that we are already on our way. We call this the 'endowed progress effect':

👍 **Do**
Gifted progress.

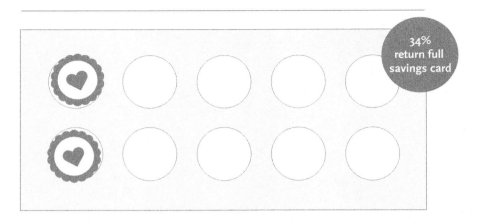

👎 **Don't**
Start with a blank card.

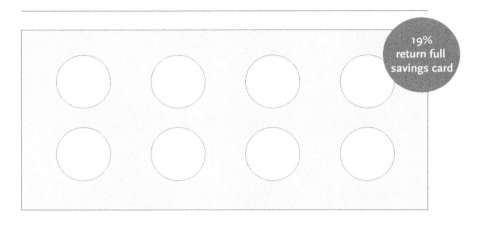

Use a mini form

If your form consists of five or fewer fields, you may want to consider placing it directly on your landing page. A mini form on which all fields and the send button are immediately visible feels simple. Moreover, *the expected effort is lower than when you see just a button without a form (*see the *Anticipated Effort* chapter in Part 4):

👍 Do

Mini form on the landing page.

👎 Don't

A button on the landing page and a mini form on new page.

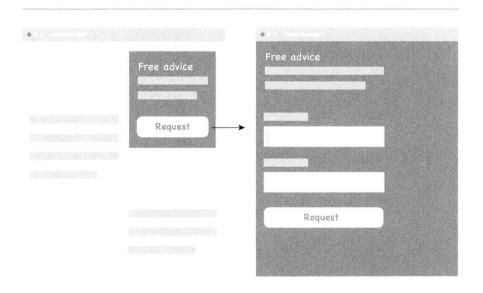

A mini form works especially well for lead generation, where visitors only leave their contact details and do not buy anything yet. Do not use this strategy for ordering products online as it requires more information from your visitor. In addition: a well-designed checkout, where you can check the ordered product and adjust it if necessary, generates much more confidence than a mini form.

Make configuration easy

In some checkouts, visitors first have to make certain choices to configure your product or service. Think of designing a sneaker, putting together a chest of drawers, or configuring an e-bulletin. In such cases, open your checkout with the configuration and only ask visitors for their personal details later. Designing or composing something is much more fun and safe than entering personal data. It is a smaller commitment than revealing your personal details.

Always make configurations easy. You could use the following three strategies, for example (see also the eponymous chapters in part 4):

Select defaults
Pre-fill the most likely option.

Reduce options
Make sure that visitors do not experience any choice stress. If each step consists of no more than five choices, you're all set. If there are more choices, it's best to hide them behind a click:

👍 **Do**
Hide less popular options behind a click.

👎 **Don't**
Show too many options at once.

Make your choice

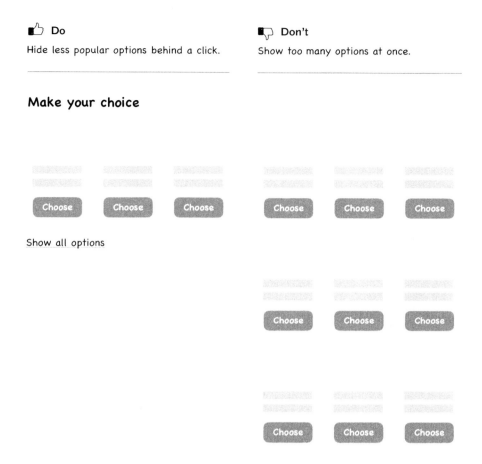

Show all options

Offer decision assistance
Explain each step. Hide the explanation behind a click to keep things organized:

👍 **Do**

Provide decision aid for steps that require a choice.

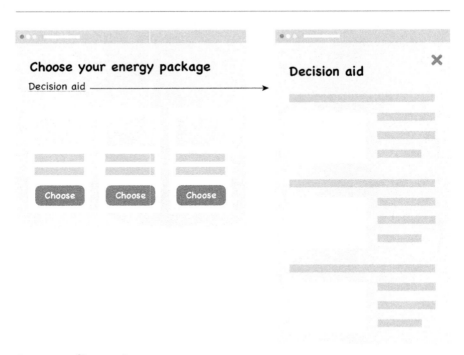

Remove distractions

If you want to seal the deal quickly, your checkout should not contain any distractions. (See the *Remove Distractions* chapter in part 4.) There are three easy ways to do this:

Remove competing prompts

Remove any links to other parts of your online environment, as they only serve to compete for attention. For example, do not use the checkout to promote your newsletter. Attempts at upselling (like bargains) can also harm your conversion.

Remove navigation

Large webshops remove the navigation in their checkout, so that visitors can only return to the homepage via the logo. This is a classic example of how to make unwanted behavior more difficult.

Remove unnecessary content

Any content that does not contribute to facilitating the checkout will only distract from the goal. So, don't blabber on about your company, the charities you support, or your latest usability award.

In the Amazon checkout there is only one prompt: the order button. The progress bar, and even the logo, are not clickable.

Use an order summary box that keeps track of everything

During the checkout, your visitors make their choices and enter their details. The closer they get to the final buying decision, the more they switch to System 2. That means that their mind becomes sharper, and doubt may strike, which may lead to questions they hadn't thought of before.

For example, questions about the product itself:

- Will this product fit through the mailbox?
- Can I cancel this subscription on a monthly basis?

There may be questions about previously made choices:

- Did I select the correct size?
- Did I choose the correct starting date?

Your visitor may have questions about the information they have just entered:

- Did I spell my name right?
- Have I entered the correct telephone number?

You always want to avoid your visitors having to leave the checkout to find an answer to their question, which is why a so-called order summary box is a handy solution. It contains information about all the choices visitors have made so far. This gives System 2 the opportunity to check the entered data.

A good order summary box is always visible, folds out on small screens, and contains links to product information. But beware: do not link visitors directly to the product detail page. Always keep them in the checkout. Create a pop-up or detail screen with a link back to the checkout:

Make every choice customizable

While going through the checkout, your visitor may suddenly start to have doubts about previously made choices. A different size? A different delivery address? Order as a gift? Design your checkout in such a way that visitors can easily change these things without having to start all over again.

You can do this, for example, by putting a change link next to every detail in the order summary box. You can also make sure that visitors can easily go back one step to change their details. Make sure your website or app 'remembers' the entered data, so you don't burden your visitors with double the work.

Help your visitors to anticipate

Checking out is a System 2 task, but that doesn't mean System 1 is absent. That's why it is a good idea to let your visitors anticipate the pleasure they will experience when they have purchased your product or service during checkout. This allows you to use the future reward to maintain their diligent completing behavior during the checkout. (See the *Anticipatory enthusiasm* chapter in Part 3.)

You can do this, for example, by showing a nice image of the product. Please note: the thumbnail in the order summary box is usually too small to really create 'wanting' and boost dopamine levels.

You can also help your visitors anticipate their future rewards with copy. Keep it short and simple, to increase the chance that your text will actually be read. A few examples:

- **The reward immediately after confirmation**
  In one minute, you'll have access to all our learning resources.
  We will email you your ticket immediately.
  Our delivery person will be at your door in the morning.

- **How your visitor will benefit from your product or service**
  This bike is practically maintenance-free.
  You will love the image quality.
  Reading this book is going to save you a lot of time.

Communicate reversibility

The best cure for uncertainty about a decision is the idea that you can still reverse it. If this is the case in your situation, make this clear in the vicinity of the confirm button:

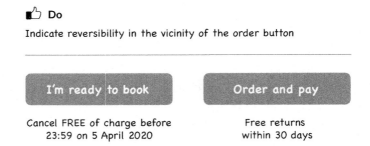

👍 **Do**

Indicate reversibility in the vicinity of the order button

Make it clear what the next step is

Explain where your visitors are going next in the checkout button texts. This gives them a sense of control and reduces their stress and uncertainty:

👍 **Do**

Clearly indicate the next step during checkout.

👎 **Don't**

Use button texts like 'Continue', leaving people unsure where they are going next.

In this example, the text under *Do* is much longer than under *Don't*, even though we've been going on about the shortest possible texts. What's that all about?

Well, earlier in the book, we talked about advertising and communicating with System 1. In the checkout, on the other hand, you are dealing with concentrated visitors. In other words, System 2 is running at full speed. At this point, predictability is more important than brevity. (If you can trim a text while maintaining predictability, you should, of course, do just that.)

Eliminate uncertainty

During checkout, your visitors may suddenly be overcome by doubt. The minute you can remove these doubts, you increase the chance of conversion. You can do this, for example, by removing the uncertainty with reassuring texts:

Your visitor's uncertainty	Reassuring texts
Will returns be a hassle?	Easy returns, no questions asked.
Will I be stuck for an entire year?	Can be canceled immediately at any time.
Am I going to get nuisance calls for the rest of my life?	We will call only once to schedule an appointment.

You can include this microcopy in your order summary box, for example, or near the confirmation button.

Do not make registration mandatory

Large webshops like Amazon require their visitors to create an account before they can order. Although we recommend studying the online environment of these types of companies, we advise against copying this particular requirement. Creating an account may seem like only a minor effort and can offer you advantages, but psychologically, 'registering' and 'not registering' are different customer experiences. Take this statement from a user test, for example.

> *'I've come here to buy something, not for a long-term relationship.'*

Web design guru Jared Spool claims to have earned $300 million in additional sales by changing the 'Register' button into a 'Continue'[51] button, so registering was no longer required to be able to order. Other cases also show that offering checkout without registration generates more sales.

Hide the discount code field behind a click

If visitors who don't have a discount code come across a field where they have to enter a discount code, they might think that others can buy the same product for a lower amount. This reduces the perceived value of the product. In addition, it is a prompt to go and search for a code somewhere else on the Internet, at which point they navigate away from the checkout. In terms of the Fogg Behavior Model, this means that the discount code field is harmful at both the prompt and motivation level.

The lucky people who do have a discount code should be able to enter it, of course. However, don't make the discount code field too conspicuous and make sure people have to open it before they can enter their code. You don't need to worry about this field being difficult to find; people who have a discount code are motivated to find it, and they won't mind going through the trouble of that extra click:

Do
Hide the discount code behind a click.

 Don't
Use a discount field that draws too much attention, making people feel like they need to enter a discount code.

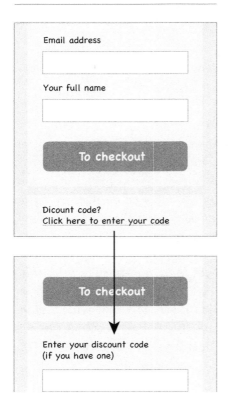

Communicate scarcity, even during checkout

According to Robert Cialdini, scarcity really motivates us to make decisions. His advice is to communicate scarcity, particularly at the end of the buying process, to increase motivation to take that last step. Even if you already communicated scarcity on the product detail page, don't hesitate to repeat it during checkout.

Displaying the limited time your visitors have to order is a good form of scarcity to apply during checkout, by letting people know how many minutes you will 'hold' the product for them:

Please note that visitors may experience this form of scarcity as irritating, especially when combined with a countdown clock. Think carefully about whether it suits your brand. If it does and it works, no problem.

Tell visitors what will happen after the last click

Even at the very last step of the checkout – once your visitors have entered all their details – uncertainty can still strike. People start wondering: what happens when I press the order button? That is why it is a good idea to explain under the buy button what happens after that last click:

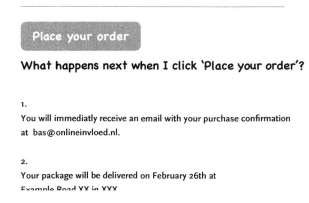

Use the thank-you page as the start for a new behavior

The thank-you or confirmation page is the page that visitors see once the deal has been closed. If you want to offer excellent service, you should at least do the following:

- thank your customer;
- explain what is going to happen next;
- tell them what you do and do not expect from them.

Good behavior designers see the thank-you or confirmation page as a successful ending, as well as a new beginning. It is the perfect place for a prompt that asks for a new behavior. After all, you have the full attention of your visitor, who is in a positive mood to boot. So, consider which behavior you wish to see as a follow-up:

- ordering an additional product;
- completing your profile;
- registering for the newsletter;
- sharing with friends;
- creating an account.

It may be tempting to offer all these prompts at the same time, but beware: prompts that compete with each other are less successful than one prompt that gets the focus. (See the *Competing prompts* chapter in Part 2.)

Prompt to encourage your visitor to go back to the shopping cart

Despite all your efforts to apply all the principles and strategies, a large proportion of your visitors will leave your shopping cart without paying. You can send them an 'abandoned shopping cart email' as a prompt to come back – provided you have their email address.

This type of email has two major advantages: it is free, and it reaches motivated people. This type of email makes it easier for them to return to the checkout and show the desired behavior.

HOW TO APPLY BEHAVIORAL PSYCHOLOGY

Conversion research

This book is about applying psychology to the design of your online environment. All the design principles we cover are based on the psychological properties that every human being basically possesses. This includes your customers. If you want to design the perfect webshop, sales funnel or customer journey, however, you also have to look for insights that apply mainly and exclusively to your specific product, service, or customer.

What about, for example, the motivation and ability of visitors to your website? Chances of finding scientific research on this specifically, are minimal. By doing your own research, you can discover, in concrete terms, what you want to know about your online environment.

For many of our assignments, our clients send us research reports full of interesting information. But in most cases, this information was not useful for our mission: increasing conversion. These reports tend to paint a picture of the quality of an online environment, and often include questions like:

- How satisfied are visitors?
- How easily can they find the information they are looking for?
- What are the chances that they will recommend your website or app to others?

As a behavior designer, this kind of information isn't very useful; the fact that you score a 6.3 on 'findability of information' does not give you concrete tools to increase the desired behavior.

What you will benefit from are qualitative insights that are directly related to the desired behavior in your online journey. We can divide these insights into three categories:

- **Barriers** – What holds visitors back from behaving the way you want them to?
- **Boosters** – What motivates and stimulates visitors to do the desired behavior?
- **Information needs** – What information do visitors need to do the desired behavior?

We will discuss this in more detail in the following paragraphs.

Barriers

If you want to find out why visitors do not do the desired behavior, you have to investigate for yourself. Your ultimate goal is a list of all the reasons why visitors are not doing what you want. Why are they hesitating? Why do they choose a different provider? What are they possibly afraid of?

The principles in this book are a good starting point. Visitors often do not display the desired behavior because:

- there are too many choices at the same time;
- the options are similar;
- there is too much text;
- there is a lack of trust (with unknown products);
- the structure differs from that of other websites.

You can use qualitative research to validate these barriers. In other words: checking whether they do, in fact, get in the way of the desired behavior. What's even more important: qualitative research will help you to discover any additional barriers that specifically apply to the purchase of your product or service, including barriers that you had not thought of yourself. Take a look at these examples from our own experience:

The desired behavior	Example of a barrier that we never thought of ourselves
Buying in a webshop	'I absolutely do not want my parcel to be delivered to the neighbors, but I am not sure how I can prevent this.'
Making an appointment for a new kitchen with a kitchen consultant	'I'm afraid I will get a salesperson on the line and not an expert.'
Booking a hotel package with a sauna	'I'm worried I won't be allowed to wear a swimsuit in the sauna.'

Barriers can be identified by asking potential and existing customers open questions, for example, through interviews and questionnaires, but also by asking website visitors a direct question in a pop-up window.

You can ask visitors the following questions:

- *What is stopping you from ordering the product?*
- *Why are you leaving this page?*
- *Why did you decide not to order the product?*
- *What is stopping you from making an appointment?*

You could ask existing customers the following questions:

- *Can you think of a reason why you almost didn't order the product?*
- *Can you think of any reasons why other people might drop out early?*

You could ask potential customers the following questions (e.g., via respondent agencies):

- *What would be a reason not to do it?*
- *Why would you not choose us?*

Pot of misery or pot of gold?

Making a list of all the reasons why visitors do not do what you want can be disheartening, especially when you see all those barriers listed one after the other. Better to see it as a pot of gold: systematically removing barriers is going to result in huge profits. And every barrier that you have identified and your competitor hasn't (yet) gives you a competitive edge.

Boosters

You can use boosters to encourage and motivate visitors to do the desired behavior. What really gets them going? And what is the decisive argument for choosing you? Earlier in this book, we gave you some examples of boosters, like:

- showing pictures that stimulate anticipation;
- giving positive feedback;
- showing positive reviews from people your visitors can identify with;
- making cancellation free and straightforward.

Again, use additional research to discover specific boosters for your product or service. Below are some examples from our practice:

The desired behavior	Example of a booster that we would never have come up with ourselves
Buying in a webshop	'I could have bought the product elsewhere, but I wanted to buy from you because you offered the most honest information.'
Making an appointment for a new kitchen with a kitchen consultant	'The only one who had appointment slots after 9 PM.'
Booking a hotel package with a sauna	'Clear pictures of the room you actually sleep in.'

Your happy customers are an excellent source of booster ideas. They have shown the desired behavior and are probably willing to give you their reasons for this behavior. A few examples of questions you can ask existing customers:

- *Why did you choose this product?*
- *What was the decisive argument for doing so?*
- *What motivated you to choose us?*

Social Proof
Tracking down boosters with existing customers has another major advantage: you can use their reasons to choose you or your products as 'customer quotes' on your website – with their permission, of course. This gives you an instant persuasive form of social proof.

Information needs

Our last category of qualitative insights is all about your visitors' information needs. What do they need to know before they can say yes? At the beginning of this practical part, we already discussed which information plays a role in online persuasion. This information includes answers to questions such as:

- What exactly are the total costs?
- What does the delivery process look like?
- What happens when I click 'Order'?
- How can I cancel afterward?

In addition, visitors need to know certain things that are specific to your product or service to aid conversion. That is why we also give three examples from our practice here:

The desired behavior	Example of a need for information that we had not thought of ourselves
Buying in a webshop	'How long is the power cord?'
Making an appointment for a new kitchen with a kitchen consultant	'How can I optimally prepare for the consultation?'
Booking a hotel package with a sauna	'Can I check in after midnight?'

Just like with barriers and boosters, you can identify information needs by asking open questions. What kind of questions you should ask, depends on whom you're asking.

You could ask respondents:

- *What do you need to know before you can say yes?*

Ask participants in a usability test:

- *What is the first bit of information you look for?*

Ask visitors:

- *Are you missing any information on this page?*

Ask existing customers:

- *Looking back, is there anything you wish you had known before?*
- *What information was missing that might not have made you a customer?*

Analyze your search function

If you have a search function on your site, you can put it to good use to find out more about your visitors' information needs. All it takes is a good look at what they enter in the search field. When a search term keeps coming back, it often means that information is missing or people can't find it quickly enough.

HOW TO APPLY BEHAVIORAL PSYCHOLOGY
Web analysis

In addition to qualitative research, it is a good idea to look at quantitative data about the use of your online environment. You can do this with Google Analytics or other web analytics software.

Web analysis is a profession in its own right, and many excellent books have been written about it. As behavior designers, our main task is to provide insight into where most visitors drop out and who exactly they are.

Chart the drop-out rates for each individual step
If you want to make this transparent, it's best to map out for each step in the customer journey what percentage of visitors drop out and what percentage clicks through. Doing so will help you to trace any bottlenecks pretty quickly. Below is a concrete example to show you how analysis of your drop-out rates can help improve your online environment.

Suppose your customer journey starts with an email, followed by a landing page and then the checkout. If it turns out that 75 percent of your visitors click through to the checkout from the landing page, but only 1 percent then convert, it could be one of two things.

Your first thought is probably that the landing page is fine but there is something wrong with the checkout. There is a good chance that this is the case. Possible causes include conversion killers in your checkout, like a discount code field that attracts too much attention, or sudden (and, therefore, unexpected) additional costs.

However, what also often happens is that visitors cannot find certain information about a product or service on the landing page. They hope to find out more during checkout, but when this doesn't happen, they drop out. So, basically, things already went wrong on the landing page.

It's important to understand that you cannot draw unambiguous conclusions from quantitative data alone. That is why the best conversion specialists always use a mix of quantitative and qualitative research.

Segment customers
Our advice is to segment your dropouts, for example, by looking at the type of device they use (desktop, tablet, mobile) and how they ended up in your online environment (via an advertising campaign or directly).

If the percentage of click-throughs on mobile devices is much lower than on desktops, there is probably something wrong with your mobile website. And if visitors arriving via one advertising campaign convert much less often than those from another, you may be promising something that you don't deliver on in your online environment.

Look at benchmarks
When analyzing your data, also look at the average percentages in your industry. If you have a 10 percent conversion rate while the norm in your industry is 5 percent, it's going to be difficult to increase it to 15 percent. If you're at 1 percent and 5 percent is the average, however, then you know that your redesigning efforts are sure to pay off.

Analyze your competitors
Finally, don't fixate too much on your own site. Instead, analyze what your competitors are doing and how they have set up their website. Not only to gain inspiration but also to be aware of what your intended visitor will see there.

HOW TO APPLY BEHAVIORAL PSYCHOLOGY

Optimizing by experimenting

In this book, we have described quite a few design principles. They will help you to persuade more people to display the online behavior you want.

If you want to optimize an existing website, you can use the principles in this book to implement improvements step by step. A popular way to do this is through A/B testing, where software randomly divides your visitors into two groups: A and B. Group A is shown your original online environment; group B gets the modified version. This allows you to verify whether a principle actually works for your situation. For example:

- variant A (original) – without social proof;
- variant B (experiment) – with social proof.

Version A
The origional without social proof.

Email address

yourname@example.com

Subscribe

You can always unsubscribe with one click

Version B
Possible optimization with social proof.

Email address

yourname@example.com

10,202 internet professionals receive new insights every week.

Subscribe

You can always unsubscribe with one click

When is your test successful?
Only 10-20 percent of all A/B tests performed worldwide deliver positive results. Our experience is that the principles and ways of thinking in this book – if properly applied – can increase the percentage of 'winners' to 40-50 percent.

If your test doesn't generate any differences, it may mean that your design adjustment doesn't make any difference to your conversion rate, or that the effect is so small that it is simply not measurable. If this happens and you are sure that variant B is more user-friendly than variant A (or in BJ Fogg's terms: increases ability), we advise you to make the change.

If variant B consists of adding motivation-enhancing content (such as authority or social proof) and this does not result in additional conversion, it is best to continue using variant A. In our experience, simplicity is always better. Avoiding superfluous content on your site creates space for future ideas that do yield results.

Only start if you have enough conversion
You can find many good manuals on A/B testing online. One prerequisite for performing this type of test properly is that you have enough conversions to get a statistically significant result. Experts say you need a thousand conversions per month to be able to do solid A/B testing. In other words: a thousand products sold, a thousand registrations or a thousand other final conversions that you aim for.

If you have less than a thousand conversions per month, you can still only detect larger differences in conversion between A and B. You can also score big time with the principles in this book. So, don't let this high number discourage you, and start an experiment.

Rate only based on final conversions
We often see that A/B testers do not focus on the final conversion but on intermediate steps. One example of an intermediate step is the number of visitors who click through to checkout from a landing page. Let's say you measure the following:

- variant A – 50 percent click-through to checkout;
- variant B – 55 percent click-through to checkout.

You might think that B is the better option and that you should substitute B for A for all your visitors. But if you continue your analysis, you may encounter the following:

- variant A – 10 percent complete checkout and pay;
- variant B – 9 percent complete checkout and pay.

In the end, A is a little better, because if you consider the final conversions, the numbers look like this:

- variant A – 5.00 percent conversion (10 percent of 50 percent);
- variant B – 4.95 percent conversion (9 percent of 55 percent).

Effects like these are relatively common in practice. In this example, the underlying reason for the lower score of variant B could be that visitors click through too quickly and miss out on essential information, which they can then no longer easily find in the checkout. This causes a delay, which then results in some of the visitors dropping out.

Make a hypothesis

The principles in this book are ideally suited to formulate a science-based hypothesis. This means that you use the A/B test to prove whether a hypothesis is true or false. This is much more favorable than random testing without having an idea of why something might work.

Here is an example of a hypothesis you can formulate with the principles of this book:

> *Research shows that potential customers may drop out when faced with choice stress. We expect that reducing the number of choices on the page will increase clicks and, ultimately, conversion too.*

Another example:

> *Since we are an unknown brand, gaining trust is important. We expect that adding social proof in the form of three testimonials and logos of well-known customers will lead to a higher conversion from visitor to lead.*

New environment

So far, we have talked about optimizing an existing website step by step. But you can also use A/B testing to design something completely new. To do this, you go live with different variants, and after a week or two you will know which one works best. This will then be your final version.

Incidentally, the idea is not to suggest A/B testing at every design meeting. A/B testing is expensive because it is very time-consuming. You can make many design decisions without experimenting, based on the principles of this book and your own research.

A/B testing for a new website

You may want to consider an A/B test for a brand new website if the theory yields different ideas that do not combine well. We'll discuss three such situations:

1. design trade-offs;
2. different prompt strategies;
3. the first impression on your landing page.

A/B testing design trade-offs

When design principles are incompatible, this is also called a 'trade-off'. In such cases, with the current state of science, it is impossible to predict what will work best for you.

The most important trade-offs are principles that simultaneously increase motivation and reduce ability. A few examples:

Increases conversion	Reduces conversion
Adding motivation-enhancing content (such as testimonials, countdown clocks, and pictures of unpacking moments) can increase motivation.	The page becomes longer and more complicated, so your visitor's brain has to work harder and needs more time to absorb everything. This reduces ability, in other words.
Having to make an effort to obtain something (like answering a pop-quiz question or customizing a product) can increase perceived value, and thus motivation.	Asking your visitor to put in extra effort reduces ability.

Increases conversion	Reduces conversion
The more different products you offer, the more likely it is that your visitors will find the perfect match.	The more choices we have, the greater the risk of choice stress, or even choice paralysis.
Making your product more expensive increases perceived value and motivation to possess it.	Making your product more expensive decreases the ability to buy it.

Examine which trade-off plays a role in your case and experiment to find out what will yield the most profit for you.

A/B testing prompt strategies
If you want to distract people from their activities with a prompt, you can use a prompt strategy. (See the *Curiosity, Exceptional benefit, Simple question* and *Unfinished journey* chapters in Part 2.)

You can't use these strategies all at the same time, and you don't know which one will generate the most visitors in your case. Testing different strategies against each other in an experiment will help you to find out what yields the most for you. If an exceptional advantage clearly works better than curiosity, that's what your campaign should be all about. You will then optimize that winning strategy with further A/B testing. It is a good idea, however, to test your chosen strategy against the other strategy over time, to check that it is still the best.

First impression A/B testing
You only have one chance to make a first impression, which is mainly based on the top of your page. Space here is limited to the viewport (the visible part for which you don't have to scroll). You can apply dozens of principles here, but not all of them will fit on such a small section of the screen. So, you have to make a choice.

A/B tests can help you to make that choice. For example, you can test whether authority (customer logos) works better than social proof (a testimonial). They will likely both inspire confidence, but sometimes you only have room for one of them.

Your elevator pitch is another element of the first impression. Through experimentation, you can find out if features work better than benefits, and whether you should focus on loss aversion, for example, or whether you should name the benefit.

What are the benefits?	What are the features?
Find a partner that suits you perfectly	The only dating app that matches based on OCEAN personality traits.

Loss aversion (negative)	Benefit (positive)
Never be late for meetings again	Always be on time for your appointments from now on.

Don't forget your main visual, which is perfect for A/B testing. Experiment with different persuasion strategies. Test a picture that clearly explains the product against one that shows the reward and/or one that appeals to an underlying need. (See the *Landing Pages* chapter in this part.)

HOW TO APPLY BEHAVIORAL PSYCHOLOGY
Behavior Design Roadmap

Many web designers need rules that are simple and easy to remember, for example: the button must always be red and positioned within the viewport. Reality is more complicated, however. You can actually end up way off target if you blindly follow this type of rule. We hope this book will help you look at online behavior in a more nuanced way. And that you develop the right mindset to use the Fogg Behavior Model when designing, and to think systematically about prompt, motivation, and ability.

If we look at the rule about the red button from BJ Fogg's point of view, it seems like a good choice because this kind of button stands out. But it's certainly not always the best solution. It could be that the desired micro behavior for your visitor is reading and scrolling. If that is the case, a red button inside the viewport comes too early and only distracts. And the color red will only stand out if the rest of the page doesn't feature too much red.

We have prepared a Behavior Design Roadmap to give you handles for the structured application of the theory and practical advice in this book. If you answer the questions in the second column for every step, you can be sure that you are looking at your online environment in a nuanced way. Chances are that you will give your business a significant boost.

Behavior Design Roadmap

Step	Ask yourself	Chapter
1. Determine the desired behavior		
	What is the desired behavior?	What is behavior design?
2. Investigate barriers, boosters and information needs		
	What holds your visitors back from behaving the way you want them to? What would win them over? What information do they need to be able to say yes?	Conversion research
3. If applicable: persuade your audience to go to your website or page		
	Which prompt will draw your visitors away from what they are doing? Which prompt strategy works best to achieve this?	What is a prompt?
	a) Can you arouse curiosity?	Curiosity
	b) Can you name an extraordinary advantage in a maximum of five words?	Exceptional benefit
	c) Can you ask a simple question?	Simple question
	d) Can you frame the behavior as an unfinished task?	Unfinished journey
4. Design the first baby step		
	What small commitment can you ask for to start the customer journey?	Baby steps
	What is the prompt for this first behavior?	What is a prompt?
	Which soft call to action fits in with this?	Baby steps
5. Describe all the baby steps that lead to the desired behavior		
	Can you divide the behavior into small steps? What are these small steps and which prompts trigger these micro behaviors?	What is a prompt?
6. Amplify all your prompts		
If possible: remove competing prompts	Are there any competing prompts? Can you remove these competing prompts? How can your prompts attract maximum attention?	Competing prompts
Attract maximum attention	Can you add movement to your prompt? Can you make your prompt deviate more from its environment in terms of color or shape? Can you use a strong emotion? Can you use a person or animal?	Attention
Make sure the affordance is good enough	Is it clear to your visitors where they can click? Is it clear to your visitors that they can scroll?	Affordance
Use soft calls to action	Can you write the button text in a way that makes it seem like a smaller commitment?	Baby steps
Name the desired behavior, literally	Can you express the prompt in the imperative?	Name the desired behavior, literally
If necessary: generate extra stopping power for your follow-up prompts	Can you apply a prompt strategy (see step 3)?	

Behavior Design Roadmap

Step	Ask yourself	Chapter
7. Analyze the motivation		
Walk through all the steps you want your visitors to take, and decide where you need to boost their motivation (i.e. wherever the behavior is difficult)	Is it clear to your visitors what the benefit is? If the benefit is not clear: are you communicating this benefit sufficiently clearly and concisely? How motivated are your visitors at every step? Which steps are difficult and cannot be made easier? Can you increase the motivation here?	What is motivation?
8. Use motivation-boosting principles		
Help your visitors to anticipate	Can you describe the future moments of happiness that your visitors may experience as a result of the desired behavior? Can you visualize these 'rewards' realistically, to increase the anticipation?	Anticipatory enthusiasm
Appeal to basic needs	On what basic human needs is your visitors' motivation based? Can you come up with images that appeal to these needs?	Appealing to basic needs
Show social proof, especially at the beginning, to gain confidence	How can you show that other people who are like your visitors also do the behavior? How can you make your social proof more credible?	Social proof
Show your authority, this is also important to gain trust	How can you demonstrate that you are an authority? Can you show diplomas? Can you refer to any blogs or books you have authored? Can you show any quality criteria that your products meet? Can you show how many years of work experience you have? Can you make use of borrowed authority? Can you show well-known customers? Can you show the beautiful building from where you work? Are there any positive reviews or reviews from authorities in your field?	Authority
Ask for small commitments	Can you divide big, difficult steps into some smaller ones? Can you draw your visitors' attention to previous behavior so that they want to act consistent with it? Is the number of steps too big, making things daunting?	Baby steps
Communicate scarcity	How can you make use of scarcity in stock? How can you make use of scarcity of time? What would go wrong if your visitors wait longer? Can you create scarcity?	Scarcity
Create a positive mood	What positive feedback can you give after every step?	Positive feedback
Emphasize potential loss	What would your visitors lose if they decide not to do business with you? How can you apply loss language?	Loss aversion
Increase the perceived value	Can you get your visitors to make a small effort to increase the perceived value? Can you show how much and what effort you put into your product or service?	Perceived value
Use reasons why	Can you think of reasons why your visitors should do the desired behavior?	Reasons why

Behavior Design Roadmap

Step	Ask yourself	Chapter
9. Make the desired behavior as easy as possible		
Look at the desired behavior and analyze how you can simplify it	Can you reduce the mental effort? Can you reduce the physical effort? Can you lower the price, split it into micro payments or make the purchase feel cheaper? Can you save your visitors time? Can you make the behavior look like something your visitors are already used to doing? Can you make the behavior less socially uncomfortable?	
10. Use principles to minimize mental effort		
Use as little text as possible	Can you use fewer words without losing meaning or persuasiveness?	The Jenga technique
Kill your darlings: avoid or remove unnecessary distractions	Is there anything that distracts from the desired behavior? Can you eliminate it?	Removing distractions
Fill in as much data as possible	What information can you fill in for your visitors in advance? For which fields can you fill in suggestions?	Default, prefill and autocomplete
Provide a clear page structure	Are the principles of hierarchy, rhythm, columns and juxtaposition in order?	Page structure
Don't ask your visitors to think or make calculations unnecessarily	Can you avoid unnecessary jargon, thinking and calculations?	
Give clear feedback everywhere	Is it clear to your visitors what effect an action has had? Can you express negative feedback positively and gratefully?	Provide feedback
Make sure steps are reversible	Can your visitors undo choices and decisions? Do you communicate this reversibility clearly and in advance?	Offer reversibility
Use design patterns that your visitors know inside out	Do you use design patterns everywhere that visitors are used to?	Familiarity
Minimize the anticipated effort	Can you reduce the anticipated effort?	Anticipated effort
	If so, how can you communicate the anticipated effort as 'small'?	
Make undesirable behavior more difficult	What behavior do you want to discourage? How can you make this behavior more difficult?	Make unwanted behavior more difficult
11. Make choosing easier		
Analyze all the steps where your visitors are asked to make a choice	Where do your visitors need to choose from multiple options?	
Reduce the number of options	Can you leave out options altogether? Can you show some of the options and hide the rest behind a click? Can you get your visitors to choose from categories first?	Offer decision aid
Design a decision aid for difficult choices	What information can you provide for the different choices? Can you design a quick filter? Can you design a wizard that offers advice based on questions?	Offer decision aid
Set a default	What is the most likely option for your visitors? In other words: what is an option that you would like your visitor to choose? Can this option be pre-selected?	Default, prefill and autocomplete

Behavior Design Roadmap

Step	Ask yourself	Chapter
12. Guide your visitors' choices		
Analyze the steps in the customer journey where you want to guide the choice	Which choices do you want to influence? Which choices are the most favorable for you and your visitors? Is the choice you guide them towards ethical?	
See which principles you can use to influence your visitors' choices		
Add a secondary option when there is only one option	What second option can you offer in addition to the option that corresponds to the desired behavior? How do you ensure that this second option gets less visual emphasis than the first?	Hobson +1
Use contrast/anchoring	Can you make sure your value feels higher or lower by working with contrasting values right before or in the vicinity?	Anchoring
Place the desired options in the middle of the choice set	Are the desired options not on the outside of the choice set? Can you add extreme options, to move the options you want to the center?	Extreme aversion
Use a decoy	Can you add an 'ugly brother' to your choice set to make the 'normal brother' look more attractive?	Decoy
Nudge desired choices	Can you give your visitors a subtle push in the direction of one or two choices you want?	Nudging

Disclaimer

This book does not cover all the principles to improve prompts, motivation, and ability. We have made a selection of principles that have resulted in many winning ideas in our practice. We have not included principles that, in our view, have proved to be irrelevant, even if you encounter them in many other places.

Finally

We hope this book will help you to look at human behavior in a scientific and systematic way. Start by thinking of behavior as a combination of a prompt, motivation, and ability, and always wonder how you can systematically influence it with design and content. Then conduct continuous experiments to see what works best for your online environment and your target audience. In other words, don't randomly try things or copy what others are doing, but opt for skilfull behavior design that is rooted in psychology.

If you have any questions or feedback, please visit onlineinfluence.com for additional content, handy canvases, information about online training, and information on how to contact us. And if you have some good examples of applied influencing principles of your own, please send them to example@onlineinfluence.com or scan the QR-code below.

We love hearing from you, and you will always get a personal reply.

We wish you the best of luck in increasing your online results. See you soon!

Bas Wouters
Joris Groen

Checklists for the different applications

To make your life easier, we have translated the tips from Part 6 (*How to apply behavioral psychology*) into checklists. We have discussed every technical term that you come across in this book. We recommend that you read the book first to get the most out of it.

We'll talk about the following:

- general online advertising
- display ads
- social media ads
- email ads
- landing pages
- product detail pages
- checkouts

General online advertising checklist

- ☐ Is the cost model clear?
- ☐ Are you using a prompt strategy that fits the cost model?
    - ☐ If you pay per view (CPM): Curiosity
    - ☐ If you pay per view (CPM): Simple question
    - ☐ For each cost model (CPM, CPC, CPA): Exceptional benefit
- ☐ Can you use fewer words without losing meaning or persuasiveness?
- ☐ Can System 1 understand the text?
- ☐ Is there a single, clear call to action?
- ☐ Is there enough affordance to click or swipe?

Display ads checklist

- ☐ Does your banner draw enough attention?
- ☐ Can you use movement in your banner?
  - ☐ If so, are you using a starting or looming motion for maximum attention?
- ☐ Is there enough affordance to click or swipe?
- ☐ Are you creating stopping power through one of the following prompt strategies?
  Curiosity
  - ☐ If so, are you filtering the right audience if you pay per click?

  Simple question
  - ☐ If so, are you filtering the right audience if you pay per click?

  Exceptional benefit
  - ☐ If so, are you using a hard call to action if you pay per click?
  - ☐ Are you using a soft call to action if you pay per view or per conversion?
  - ☐ Are you experimenting with different calls to action to see what yields the most benefits?
- ☐ Are you using images that support the chosen prompt strategy?
- ☐ If using a video: does it contain a mini story?
- ☐ Can it be done with fewer words?
- ☐ Are you not using overly complicated words?
- ☐ Does the landing page perfectly match the advertisement?

Social media ads checklist

- ☐ Are you creating stopping power through one of the following prompt strategies?
  Curiosity
    - ☐ Are you attracting the right audience if you pay per click?
    - ☐ Is it possible not to show the price, to increase curiosity?

  Simple question
    - ☐ Are you attracting the right audience if you pay per click?

  Exceptional benefit
    - ☐ Are you showing an extremely low price or a high discount percentage?
    - ☐ Are you using a hard call to action if you pay per click?
- ☐ Is there perhaps too much text in the image of your ad?
- ☐ Does your ad not feel too much like advertising?
- ☐ Does your ad match the interests of your target audience?
- ☐ Is there a persuasive accompanying text with your ad?
- ☐ If you use lead ads: are you asking for as little personal information as possible here?

Email ads checklist

The subject line
- Are you using any of the following prompt strategies in the subject line?
    - Curiosity
    - Exceptional benefit
    - Unfinished journey
- Are you using techniques to make your subject line visually stand out among the subject lines of others?
- Can you include the recipient's name in the subject line?
- Are you using words in the subject line that attract attention, such as something emotional or something bizarre?
- Can it be done in fewer words without losing persuasiveness?
- Can you use shorter words?
- Are you using the name of a person in the sender field?

The content of your email
- Are you choosing one of the following two formats?
    - A single message with a clear call to action
    - A list of multiple topics and a clear call to action per topic
- If you have a list of multiple topics: does this list have a persuasive title that encourages people to go through the list?
- Does the list have a visual rhythm that makes it easy to recognize when one part ends and the next starts?
- Are you using a prompt strategy for every message?
    - Curiosity
    - Exceptional benefit
    - Simple question
    - Unfinished journey
- Can the text be even shorter?
- Are you using soft calls to action?
- Are you using a visual that supports the prompt strategy?

Landing pages checklist

- ☐ Is there a soft landing?
- ☐ Is there a clear elevator pitch?
  - ☐ For a known product: are you mentioning distinctive features?
  - ☐ For a new or unknown product: are you explaining clearly what it is?
  - ☐ Will someone who doesn't know your product understand what you mean in five seconds?
- ☐ On your landing page, are you listing the three most relevant benefits or reasons to say yes?
- ☐ Are you increasing confidence by using social proof?
- ☐ If your brand is not well-known, are you increasing the confidence by using external authority?
- ☐ Are you radiating authority with a neat visual design?
- ☐ Does your page consist of a single column?
- ☐ Is there a visual rhythm that makes it clear where a block ends and where a new block begins?
- ☐ Is it clear to your visitors that they can scroll further?
- ☐ Does the title of each block invite to read, for example, by applying a prompt strategy?
- ☐ Can the page be shorter without sacrificing persuasiveness?
- ☐ Are the details hidden behind a click?
- ☐ After reading the details, can you go back to where you left off with one click?
- ☐ Is there a clear call to action?
- ☐ Does that call to action come at the right time?
- ☐ Is your call to action sticky, so visitors can always decide to click?
  - ☐ If not, do you occasionally repeat your call to action if your page is longer than three blocks?
- ☐ Is the call to action formulated softly enough?
- ☐ Can you add an advantage to your call to action, such as 'Order with a discount'?
- ☐ Are you sure your button text is not too long?
- ☐ Are you creating anticipation through images and texts that picture the future reward for your visitor?
- ☐ Are you appealing to basic needs with images and texts that show the long-term impact of your product?
- ☐ Are you using visuals that explain how your product or service works?
- ☐ If you use video: is it clear in advance what the video is about and how long it lasts? Do you get to the point in your video quickly enough? In other words: make sure that you don't show a long intro without content.
- ☐ Can you answer yes to the questions above for both desktop and mobile versions?

Product detail pages checklist

- [ ] Does your product detail page meet landing page requirements? (See the landing pages checklist.)
- [ ] Are you answering questions about the buying process?
  - [ ] Is it clear when your product will be delivered or when your service can be used?
  - [ ] Is it clear how your product or service is delivered?
  - [ ] Is it clear what the visitor needs to do to have the product delivered or to use your service?
- [ ] Is it clear what the final price is?
- [ ] Is it clear what the possible additional costs are?
- [ ] Is it clear how and when your visitors can pay?
- [ ] Does the page contain information about you as a provider, if you are not very well-known?
  - [ ] Is it clear what kind of company you are?
  - [ ] Is it clear what you stand for?
  - [ ] Is it clear who your customers are?
  - [ ] Is it clear how long you've been around?
- [ ] Have you also answered any other questions visitors might have?
- [ ] Have you researched what questions these may be?
- [ ] Do you have a chatbot or live chat to answer any questions immediately?
- [ ] Does your page contain reviews or testimonials?
- [ ] Does your page contain a summary of the reviews or testimonials and a link to a detail page that lists them all?
- [ ] Do your pages contain product photos?
  - [ ] Can your visitors see details?
  - [ ] Are there also pictures of a person using the product?
  - [ ] Does this person match your target audience?
  - [ ] Are you using the cheerleader effect to increase the perceived value of your product?
- [ ] Is it possible to include the delivery costs in the price without making your product seem unjustifiably more expensive than a possible competitor's product?
- [ ] Are you spending as few pixels as possible on displaying the price?
- [ ] Are you using the from/for price as an anchor?
- [ ] Are you increasing the perceived value of any free extras?
- [ ] Are you sure your product detail page is not too different from that of frequently visited webshops?

- ☐ Is all this information really on your product detail page, so that your visitor doesn't have to surf back and forth?
- ☐ Are you communicating a limited supply, if there is one?
- ☐ Are you communicating the deadline for any temporary discounts?
- ☐ Are you communicating the deadline for the earliest possible delivery?
- ☐ Are you communicating scarcity in the vicinity of your call to action?
- ☐ Are you using a soft call to action? (For example: 'Add to cart').
- ☐ If you have a temporary promotion: are you using a hard call to action? (For example: 'Order now').
- ☐ Are you using a secondary call to action (such as 'Add to wish list') in the vicinity of your primary call to action?
- ☐ Are you using shortcuts for people who want to proceed quickly to the checkout with a single product?
- ☐ Can you answer yes to the questions above for both desktop and mobile versions?

Checkout checklist

- [ ] Have all links to other pages been removed?
- [ ] Is it possible to go through the checkout without mandatory registration?
- [ ] Are any long forms divided into three (maximum five) steps?
    - [ ] Have the first or the first two steps already been completed when your visitor reaches the checkout? In other words: are you offering progress as a gift to increase motivation?
    - [ ] Are you sure your progress bar is not too complicated for mobile screens?
- [ ] Are you asking for easy and less personal information first?
- [ ] Are you sure you are only asking for the information you need to reach a deal?
- [ ] Can you move data inquiries until after the deal?
- [ ] Are you using prefill as much as possible?
- [ ] Have you set a default for every choice your visitor is asked to make?
- [ ] Are you offering decision aid for difficult choices?
- [ ] Have you hidden less likely choices behind a click?
- [ ] Is it possible to see and adjust all choices visitors have made without leaving the checkout?
- [ ] Do the button texts clearly indicate what the next step is?
- [ ] Are you continuing to motivate your visitor with compliments and encouragements after every step?
- [ ] If applicable, is the discount code field hidden behind a click?
- [ ] Are you helping your visitor to anticipate the future reward, by continuing to show it and by using copy that indicates what wonderful things your visitor can expect?
- [ ] Are you indicating in advance what happens after confirming or ordering?
- [ ] Are you communicating reversibility?
- [ ] Are you removing any uncertainties with micro copy close to the button your visitor uses to confirm definitively?
- [ ] Are you using a countdown clock to increase the pressure of time for a temporary benefit? Have you tested whether this is not counterproductive?
- [ ] Are you sure your checkout does not contain any distracting content?
- [ ] Are you using a mini form when collecting leads?
- [ ] Are you using the thank-you page as the start of a new desired behavior?
- [ ] Can you send emails to encourage visitors to return to an abandoned checkout?
- [ ] Can you answer yes to the questions above for both desktop and mobile versions?

Acknowledgements

We want to thank everyone who contributed to the wonderful field of applied psychology. In particular, we would like to thank the heroes of the trade below. It was an honor to stand on your shoulders while writing this book.

Robert Cialdini
Gregory Neidert
BJ Fogg
Daniel Kahneman
Dan Ariely
Donald Norman
Jakob Nielsen

In addition, we benefited enormously from the support and involvement of the people below. A big thanks to you, too!

Natalie Bowler-Geerinck
For deep-diving into the subject matter and translating this book from Dutch to English.

Jaap Janssen Steenberg and **Stijn Kling**
For your advice, professionalism, and boundless dedication.

Wieke Oosthoek and **Elke Vergoossen**
For your advice, ideas and congenial guidance.

Olaf Igesz
For your support and unconditional belief in this project.

Victor van Loon
For always being there.

Marthe
For all your support and feedback.

Benjamin
For all your patience with Daddy.

Reading suggestions

If you want to delve deeper into the psychology of persuasion, we recommend the books below.

Robert Cialdini
Influence – The Psychology of Persuasion

Robert Cialdini
Pre-Suasion – A Revolutionary Way to Influence and Persuade

BJ Fogg
Tiny Habits – The Small Changes That Change Everything

Daniel Kahneman
Thinking, Fast and Slow

Dan Ariely
Predictably Irrational – The Hidden Forces That Shape Our Decisions

Donald Norman
The Design of Everyday Things

For all online sources, please visit **onlineinfluence.com**.

About the authors

Joris Groen
As a psychologist, Joris specialized in translating human sciences into practical design guidelines for the digital world. He worked as a user experience designer for leading agencies, companies, and brands.

In 2012, Joris founded Buyerminds, an internationally operating agency in the field of behavior design. With Buyerminds, he designed and improved hundreds of websites, webshops, apps, emails, and online campaigns. The starting point was always a scientific approach based on behavioral psychology, research and data.

In addition to managing design teams, Joris has trained hundreds of students and professionals worldwide, including web designers, user experience designers, online marketers and product owners from Coca-Cola, KLM, Alibaba, and bol.com, among others. Nowadays, he designs for Booking.com and offers online training via Onlineinfluence.nl.

Bas Wouters
As a young serial entrepreneur, Bas successfully applied persuasion science in the financial sector, where he was able to achieve sales increases of up to 500 percent. He was also successful online with Keukenplaats.nl, a disruptive lead generator in the kitchen sector, yielding millions worth of annual sales.

After selling his businesses, Bas became an apprentice to the world-renowned persuasion psychologist Robert Cialdini. Since 2017, he can proudly call himself the only Cialdini Method Certified Trainer (CMCT) in the Netherlands. Bas has coached and trained hundreds of professionals worldwide to increase their offline and online persuasion. His mission: to help people and companies attain a better level of performance by teaching them to apply principles of persuasion and behavioral science. Nowadays, Bas offers keynote talks, training, and online courses via Onlineinvloed.nl.

Bibliography

1 Leech J (2018). Psychology for designers: how to apply psychology to web design and the design process. Bristol: Mr Joe Press.
2 Fogg BJ (2019). Tiny habits: the small changes that change everything. Boston: Houghton Mifflin Harcourt.
3 Zaltman G (2003). How customers think: essential insights into the mind of the market. Boston: Harvard Business School Press.
4 Kahneman D (2011). Thinking, fast and slow. New York: Farrar, Straus and Giroux.
5 Cialdini RB (2007). Influence: the psychology of persuasion. New York: Harper Collins.
6 *See* note 5.
7 *See* note 5.
8 Cialdini RB (2016). Pre-suasion: a revolutionary way to influence and persuade. New York: Simon & Schuster.
9 Rayson S (2017). We analyzed 100 million headlines. Here's what we learned (new research). Buzzsomo. Via: www.buzzsumo.com/blog/most-shared-headlines-study.
10 Norman DA (2013). The design of everyday things: revised and expanded edition. New York: Basic Books.
11 Rayson S (2017). We analyzed 100 million headlines. Here's what we learned (new research). Buzzsomo. Via: www.buzzsumo.com/blog/most-shared-headlines-study.
12 Zeigarnik BW (1927). Das Behalten erledigter und unerledigter Handlungen. Psychologische Forschung 9:1-85.
13 *See* note 5.
14 Berridge KC, Kringelbach ML (2015). Pleasure systems in the brain. Neuron 6;86(3):646-64.
15 Sapolsky RM (2018). Behave: the biology of humans at our best and worst. Penguin Books.
16 Haldeman-Julius E (2008). First hundred million: how to skyrocket your book sales with slam dunk titles. Vancouver: Angelican Press.

17 Whitman E (2009). Ca$hvertising: how to use more than 100 secrets of ad-agency psychology to make big money selling anything to anyone. Franklin Lakes, NJ: Career Press.
18 Byrnes N (2012). Behavioral economics taps power of persuasion for tax compliance. Reuters. Via: www.reuters.com/article/us-usa-tax-behavior/behavioral-economics-taps-power-of-persuasion-for-tax-compliance-idUSBRE89S0DD20121029.
19 *See* note 5.
20 *See* note 5.
21 Freedman JL, Fraser SC (1966). Compliance without pressure: the foot-in-the-door technique. Journal of Personality and Social Psychology 4(2):195.
22 Bechara A (2004). The role of emotion in decision-making: evidence from neurological patients with orbitofrontal damage. Brain and Cognition 55(1):30-40.
23 Fogg BJ, Nass C (1997). Silicon sycophants: the effects of computers that flatter. International Journal of Human-Computer Studies 46(5):551-61.
24 Kahneman D (2011). Thinking, fast and slow. New York: Farrar, Straus and Giroux.
25 Gonzales MH, Aronson E, Costanzo M (1988). Increasing the effectiveness of energy auditors: a field experiment. Journal of Applied Social Psychology 18:1046-66.
26 Edwards H (2015). The 4 emotions that make the best emotional ads [DATA]. Wordstream. Via: www.wordstream.com/blog/ws/2015/11/09/emotional-ads.
27 Langer EJ, Blank A, Chanowitz B (1978). The mindlessness of ostensibly thoughtful action: the role of "placebic" information in interpersonal interaction. Journal of Personality and Social Psychology 36(6):635-42.
28 Iyengar SS, Lepper MR (2000). When choice is demotivating: can one desire too much of a good thing? Journal of Personality and Social Psychology 79(6):995-1006.
29 Grieser S (2014). Is too much choice killing your conversion rates? [Case studies] Unbounce. Via: www.unbounce.com/conversion-rate-optimization/psychology-of-choice-conversion-rates.
30 Vasterman J (2015). Studieschuld stevig verminderd dankzij simpele nudging-trucs op aanvraagformulieren (Study debt firmly reduced thanks to simple nudging tricks on request forms) NRC. Via: www.nrc.nl/nieuws/2015/04/13/studiefinanciering-studieschuld-stevig-verminderd-1486199-a215924.
31 Krug S (2013). Don't make me think, revisited: a common sense approach to web (and mobile) usability, 3e ed. Berkeley: New Riders Publishing.
32 Nielsen J (2017). Jakob's Law of internet user experience. Nielsen Norman Group. Via: www.nngroup.com/videos/jakobs-law-internet-ux.
33 Schutz B (2015). Conversion blast: the additional link that nobody clicks on (Hobson +1 effect). Marketing Facts. Via: www.marketingfacts.nl/berichten/conversieknaller-de-extra-link-die-niemand-klikt-hobson1-effect.
34 Ariely D (2010). Predictably irrational: the hidden forces that shape our decisions (revised and expanded edition). New York: Harper.
35 Simonson I, Tversky A (1992). Choice in context: tradeoff contrast and extremeness aversion. Journal of Marketing Research 29(3):281-95.

36 Tietz M, Simons A, Weinmann M et al (2016). The decoy effect in reward-based crowdfunding: preliminary results from an online experiment. Paper presented at the 37th International Conference on Information Systems (ICIS 2016), Dublin, Ireland.
37 Ariely D (2010). Predictably irrational: the hidden forces that shape our decisions (revised and expanded edition). New York: Harper.
38 Chaffey D (2019). Average display advertising clickthrough rates: US, Europe and worldwide display ad clickthrough rates statistics summary. Smart Insights. Via: www.smartinsights.com/internet-advertising/internet-advertising-analytics/display-advertising-clickthrough-rates/.
39 Irvine M (2019). Facebook ad benchmarks for your industry [2019]. WordStream. Via: www.wordstream.com/blog/ws/2019/11/12/facebook-ad-benchmarks.
40 Campaign Monitor (2019). What is a good email click-through rate for 2019? Campaign Monitor. Via: www.campaignmonitor.com/blog/email-marketing/2019/03/what-is-a-good-email-click-through-rate-for-2019/.
41 Lambert B (2019). Google ads CPC, CPM, & CTR benchmarks Q1 2019 archive. AdStage. Via: blog.adstage.io/google-ads-cpm-cpc-ctr-benchmarks-q1-19-archive.
42 Animalz (2019). Facebook lead ads: the definitive guide. Adespresso. Via: www.adespresso.com/blog/facebook-lead-ads.
43 Trustpilot (2018). How to calculate Google Seller Ratings' effect on CTR for Google Ads. Trustpilot. Via: www.business.trustpilot.com/reviews/browsers-to-buyers/how-to-calculate-google-seller-ratings-effect-on-adwords.
44 Carlson KA, Shu SB (2013). When three charms but four alarms: identifying the optimal number of claims in persuasion settings. SRRN. Via: www.ssrn.com/abstract=2277117.
45 Fogg BJ, Soohoo C, Danielson DR et al (2003). How do users evaluate the credibility of websites? A study with 2,500 participants. DUX '03: Proceedings of the 2003 Conference on Designing for User Experiences: 1-15. Via: dl.acm.org/doi/10.1145/997078.997097.
46 Peck J, Shu SB (2009). The effect of mere touch on perceived ownership. Journal of Consumer Research 36(3):434-47.
47 Ying H, Burns E, Lin X et al (2019). Ensemble statistics shape face adaptation and the cheerleader effect. Journal of Experimental Psychology: General 148(3):421.
48 Kolenda N (z.d.). Pricing psychology. Via: www.nickkolenda.com/psychological-pricing-strategies.
49 Baymard Institute (2019). 41 cart abandonment rate statistics. Via: www.baymard.com/lists/cart-abandonment-rate.
50 Nunes JC, Drèze X (2006). The endowed progress effect: how artificial advancement increases effort. Journal of Consumer Research 32(4):504-12.
51 Spool JM (2009). The $300 Million Button. Via: articles.uie.com/three_hund_million_button.

Printed in Great Britain
by Amazon